THE WAY IT
SPOZED TO BE

INNOVATORS IN EDUCATION
SERIES EDITOR: SUSANNAH SHEFFER

The *Innovators in Education* series brings back into print books that are both historically significant and that speak directly to today's concerns. We look for books that represent important developments in educational thought and have ongoing contemporary application. In this way, the series enables readers to connect newly published books with earlier works on similar subjects and enables current discussions to be informed and enriched by some of the best available writing on educational issues.

Also available in the series:

JAMES HERNDON

THE WAY IT SPOZED TO BE

Series Editor
SUSANNAH SHEFFER

Boynton/Cook Publishers
HEINEMANN
Portsmouth, NH

Boynton/Cook Publishers
A subsidiary of Reed Elsevier Inc.
361 Hanover Street
Portsmouth, NH 03801-3912
Offices and agents throughout the world

We would like to thank those who have given their permission to include material in this book.

Library of Congress Cataloging-in-Publication Data
is on file at the Library of Congress.
0-86709-407-9

Editor: Susannah Sheffer
Cover design: Barbara Werden
Cover photo: Mel DiGiacomo/The Image Bank
Manufacturing: Louise Richardson

Printed in the United States of America on acid-free paper
01 00 99 98 97   DA   1 2 3 4 5 6

FOREWORD TO THE NEW EDITION

We all know what's "spozed" to happen in school. Teachers know it, policy makers know it, and the students certainly know it. We know it so well that when something happens that isn't the way it's spozed to be—even if it's better, even if it's staggeringly more meaningful and more encouraging of true learning—we can't see its value.

This is what Herndon's story is about. Into a junior high school full of mostly defeated and demoralized kids walks Herndon, a new teacher with very few theories about how to make a difference. Others tell him what he's spozed to do: keep order. Toward that end, keep the kids busy—but not necessarily with anything they understand, hence the repeated suggestion that Herndon have the kids copy a paragraph from the blackboard each day even though many of them can't read it.

Herndon rejects this advice in favor of something that looks chaotic and messy but is actually real and valuable. For what was in many cases the first time, the kids in his classes began to do things that actually worked. They organized reading and writing projects. Kids who hadn't read or written before began to care about being able to. By the end of the year, the kids were keeping *themselves* busy with activities that grew out of their own concerns and furthered their own development (in general, but also with regard to literacy in particular).

One example, of many, is the Slambooks: notebooks in which the kids wrote what they thought of their classmates. This wasn't a teacher's assignment, of course. Slambooks, as anyone familiar with them knows, are a classic kid-culture activity; they're the sort of thing no teacher would think up but that kids seem to think up regularly. Most of the other teachers talked only of how to get rid of these forbidden books, but Herndon saw the matter differently:

Again, I'd been in there with 9D too long; all I could see was that they'd finally come across something that needed to be written down to be successful or interesting to them, which couldn't even exist without writing, and they were doing it as enthusiastically as possible.

This is Herndon in his characteristically diffident style, letting you know almost offhandedly that he's noticed something crucial. But that's his gift. Where others saw only rebellion, Herndon saw the connection that would be the roots of true literacy learning.

And yet despite this and other such connections, despite what looks to the reader like indisputable learning and success in his classroom at the end of a difficult year, Herndon gets fired. Results are not the point. What matters is that teachers do what they're spozed to do, that they carry on with school as we know it, not that the students are actually learning in unprecedented amounts.

Herndon wrote this book thirty years ago. In a sense, it might seem as if current school reform efforts do make results the point: "We'll raise standards, we'll require that kids learn such-and-such before they graduate," these reforms promise. But such mandates fall prey to what we might call "spozed thinking" as much as anything that happened in Herndon's time. We've decided what's spozed to happen, they say, and we'll make sure that it does. A reader of this book might ask, how *can* we make sure, when Herndon's colleagues thought that what they did was a way of making sure, too? Requiring kids to keep notebooks and be graded on them might sound like a way of ensuring that certain writing standards be met, but in fact, as Herndon observed, most kids didn't do the assignments and knew almost nothing of "adverbs, how to spell, punctuation...many hadn't even learned how to read." Most of the kids *had* been receiving failing grades for years, and it's hard to see how tougher standards would have changed that.

The Slambooks, on the other hand (along with other such activities), did what no federal mandate could: they gave the kids an actual, believable, understandable reason to write and to want to get better at writing. Imagine a government mandate that said to teachers, "You *will* be attentive to where your kids actually are, to what actually excites and interests them, and you'll stop playing that familiar and futile game of telling them what's required so that they can spend a lot of time not doing it and protesting it and figuring out how to get around it, day after day and year after year."

6

Of course, no government can mandate that teachers engage in the kind of careful and sustained observation that Herndon did, nor can it ask that teachers be willing to discard old habits for untried new ones. But Herndon's example can inspire that response in people who read him. Herndon's successes were amazing and unprecedented, but they are also believable and duplicable. They're the sort of successes that other teachers—regular, everyday teachers trying to muddle through as Herndon was—ought to be able to emulate. As John Holt wrote in a review of the original edition of the book, "We are not helped by hearing how brilliant and gifted people did miracles in the classroom....But Herndon did no miracles; all he did was to get his students, after years of apathy and rebellion, to begin educating themselves. He had never taught before, and had no special training or talents; we all have it in us to do what he did—if we want to."

In the middle of the book, Herndon devotes a concise, devastating two pages to the following advice from a colleague: "If you want the goat to pull the cart," a teacher tells him, "but he doesn't want to, you hold a carrot out in front of him. He tries to reach the carrot because he does want it. In doing so he pulls the cart. If, she said with a kind of wink, if you've attached the carrot to the cart."

Herndon tries to restate the advice: "You mean, to get the student to do the assignment because of some reward he's going to get, not because he realizes that the assignment is valuable or interesting to him. You mean, the assignment itself can't be the carrot..."

The teacher smiles because Herndon understands, as indeed he does, as indeed we are all meant to. Says Herndon, "I sneaked a quick smoke, my mind filled with carrots and outrage, and arrived upstairs a bit late to greet 9D."

Herndon has been called the funniest of the school reform writers, and this book is as hilarious as any I know. It reads like a great novel, in the tradition of Salinger, Kerouac, Vonnegut. But like any great novel, it's also telling us something important about ourselves and how we got to where we are. Savor this book. Let it fill your mind with carrots and outrage and delight and fury, but above all, let it show you the way it really is for kids in school. In any discussion of reform, that's the only sensible place to start.

SUSANNAH SHEFFER

When the taxi does not move it does not move. When
you feed it gas or treat it like a dead refrigerator it does
not move. Burn it as quick as you can.

—JACK SPICER

THE WAY IT
SPOZED TO BE

(1) Ruth

We had just come out of the library from our first meeting with the principal, just the new teachers, perhaps fifteen of us. I walked down the hall with a man named Skates whom I'd just met. It was midafternoon; the hall was dark.

At least it looks like a school, I was saying, old, dark, the same brown window shades all pulled exactly three-quarters of the way down. . . . I was rather pleased about that. A real school, not one of those new ones I saw going up all over that looked like motels or bowling alleys. I was about to say that the motel-schools fooled nobody; they were still schools, and the same old crap was going to go on in them. Here, at least, everyone was notified right away by the looks of things that it was the same old crap.

Suddenly, a trio of girls burst upon us as if they had been lying in ambush. One jumped ahead, pointing a finger at me.

You a new teacher?

Uh-huh. Yes.

What grade?

All of them, it looks like.

You teach the eighth?

Yes. Eighth too.

What you teach to the eighth grade?

English. Social Studies. No, only English to the eighth grade.
The other two girls were hanging back, giggling. This girl
crowded me, standing right next to me, looking straight up. I
kept my head absurdly raised, feeling that if I bent down I'd
graze the top of her head with my chin. I kept stepping back
in order to get a look at her, and also to get away from her.
She kept moving forward; she acted as if this was her hall, she
owned it, and I, a stranger, could be interrogated at will.
She talked very loudly, smiling and grinning all the time but
still almost shouting every word, having a fine time. It was OK
with me.

What your name?

Herndon. Mr. Herndon.

OK, Mr. Hern-don, saying Hern-dawn, accent last syllable,
as I was to hear it spoken from then on by all students. OK, Mr.
Herndon, you all right. I'm gonna be in your class. You better
believe it! I'm in your class!

Well, fine, I said. Good. The two girls giggled in the background. Skates stood around, waiting. She ignored all of them;
her business was with me.

It seemed to be over. I waved my hand at her and started to
move off. She grabbed me by the arm.

I ain't done! Listen you, Mr. Herndon, my name Ruth. Ruth!
You'll hear about me, don't worry about it! And what I say,
Mr. Herndon, you don't cause me no trouble and I don't cause
you none! You hear?

That suits me, I said. Well, see you later, Ruth, girls. Skates
and I started off.

You don't cause me none, and I don't cause you none! she
yelled once more, and then the three of them took off, sprinting
down the hall away from us, laughing like hell and yelling at the
top of their lungs. Someone opened the library door and looked
out after they passed, but they had already turned the corner
and were out of sight.

The first day, sure enough, there was Ruth in my eighth
grade B class. She was absolutely the craziest-looking girl I've
ever seen. Her hair was a mass of grease, matted down flat in

some places, sticking straight out in several others. Her face was faintly Arabic, and she was rather handsome, meaning, I suppose, that her features were Caucasian in style. She was very black. Across her forehead a tremendous scar ran in a zig-zag pattern from somewhere above the hairline on her left side across to her right eye, cutting into the eyebrow. The scar was dead white. She was about five feet three inches tall, weighed maybe 115 pounds. Not thin, anyway. Her entire figure seemed full of energy and power; she was, every time I saw her, com-pletely alert and ready. She could have been any age from fifteen to twenty-five. I once tried to look up her age, there were so many rumors about her from the faculty and from other stu-dents, but that fact was absent from her file; on every sheet, the space after *Age* was simply left blank. No one knew, and apparently no one knew why it was that no one knew.

True to her word, she didn't cause me no trouble that first day. She sat at the second desk in her row and all she did was to sit there and grab all the pencils I handed out for that row and refuse to pass them back. The row burst into an uproar, de-manding their pencils. The other rows, not having thought of this themselves, yelled derisively, That row ain't gittin' any!

Please pass the pencils back, Ruth, I said, reasonably but loudly, since I wanted to be heard. In the back of my mind I was still wondering how she got in my class, or at least how she knew she was going to be in my class. The other two girls were there too, I saw.

Ruth jumped up immediately. Don't go to hollering at me! she yelled. You got plenty of pencils! You spozed to give 'em all out! They ain't your pencils! You spozed to give 'em out! I need these pencils!

The class yelled out, Whooooo-eee! Whooo-eee! They all made the same sound. Everyone stood up, laughing and yelling whooo-eee except for the kids in Ruth's row who all screamed, We ain't got no pyenculs!

I advanced on the row. Sit down! I shouted at everybody. I did have plenty of pencils, and I was going to give one to each kid in the row and forget about it. Let her keep the goddam pencils! Who cared? But as I came toward the row, Ruth suddenly flung the handful of pencils out into the room, screeched out No! and launched herself backwards into space. She actually flew through the air and landed on her back on the floor after crashing—some part of her body or head, I couldn't tell—against a desk and a kid or two. Across the room twenty kids dived, shouting, for the pencils. No trouble, I thought bitterly, and came over to get her up. That's all I could think of at the time, get this damn girl off the floor. But again, as I moved, she jumped up, full of life, and fled for the door.

You ain't sending me to Miss Bentley, nobody sending me! I go tell her myself what you done, Mr. Herndon!

Bang. She was gone. The class was still squabbling over the pencils, but not seriously, and a few were still taunting the row which didn't have none, but only halfheartedly. They were too impressed with Ruth. So was I. I passed out some more pencils, and everyone sat down and awaited excitedly the passing out of paper, enrollment cards and books.

Still, I felt betrayed. I thought she meant it, out there in the hall, about the no trouble. Perhaps the fact that I thought about it at all, took her statement seriously in that way, was the first mistake; the girl was a student in the eighth grade, I was the teacher. Period. Or again, I had been passing out pencils all day, to each class, but as it turned out I was only supposed to give them out to my first-period class. These kids had already gotten pencils in their own first period; they were receiving a bonus, a free gift. Free gifts were a mistake too.

As it turned out, she hadn't betrayed me at all. In Ruth's terms, she hadn't really caused me no trouble. Not no real trouble. That became very clear later on in the year.

(2) Meeting

In this book I'm trying to tell about my year teaching—learning to teach—in a public school, a year spent in a particular school, at a particular time, and with particular students. These particulars are my anecdote.

It is certainly the anecdote that counts. Not the moral, the point, or the interpretation. If just the particulars can be kept clear, then there will be a kind of thing made, something to see . . . the interpretations may then be as numerous as readers.

This is why I write down whatever circumstances and events I clearly remember, in such detail as I remember, including cause, effect, and consequence if possible, hopefully without extravagance of any sort. But also, to relate only what I remember. I wouldn't consider, for instance, going back to school records to look up information, or talk to people to "refresh" my memory or to find evidence of unremembered things. I have the feeling that such as I remember will suffice, and indeed will form a pattern (a unity, an anecdote), which is the kind of thing which humans, willy-nilly, find significant.

Thus: I remember the first meeting we new teachers had there in the library, right before Skates and I ran into Ruth.

Nothing much happened. It was the same sunny September

afternoon outside, but it was rather dark inside the school and the library lights were on. There were, as I said, some fifteen of us—some white, some Negro. George Washington Junior High was a Negro school—about 98 percent Negro, they had told me downtown in the district office, as if to say not entirely Negro. I had been wondering how many of the teachers would be Negroes; well, as I said, some white and some Negro. Of the new teachers, I had talked only with Skates (white) and Mr. Brooks (Negro)—as it turned out they were the two I was to come most in contact with, and the only two of my colleagues whom, at the end of the year, I could say I really knew.

I certainly remember Mr. Grisson. He told us candidly that this was his first principalship, that he expected to make mistakes himself and certainly would not be surprised if we made some too. The thing to do with mistakes, he said, was to learn from them. He told us something of his background, his interests outside of school.

We were read off the names of department heads, and informed that they were there to help us; it was also explained to us that this departmentalization did not mean that our individual freedoms to teach how we pleased would be in any way affected, but that its purpose was to assist planning so that the students at GW might have an orderly and unrepetitive progression through the grades.

The subject of discipline was mentioned, and everyone grew alert. As Skates told me later, this was where you found out what was really supposed to happen, and of course he was absolutely right. The administration was going to make statements about discipline. No doubt they had spent some time preparing what they were going to say; what we heard was that this administration wished to concentrate on the individual, on his freedom of action, learning, growth and development, and, at the same time, to promote an orderly and responsible group of children.

The plot's always the same, whispered Skates. From this perfect and impossible statement, I gathered, you were supposed to figure out the real attitude of the administration toward the behavior of students in your classrooms, with an eye to your own evaluation. That is, what degree of control you were being ordered to maintain or what degree of disturbance and chaos would be acceptable.

On that afternoon it was really made easy by Miss Bentley, the vice-principal. Miss Bentley offered us the example of the Army. The Army, she submitted, was an organization of people given certain tasks to perform. So was a school. The tasks were vital. Perhaps, she grinned, those of us old enough could remember the messed-up details, the old hurry-up-and-wait, the origin and meaning of the word SNAFU, but the overall mission was vital. The school's overall mission was the education of children. . . .

There was nothing new in any of this even then, and as a result I lost interest and failed to make interpretations. I wasn't worrying about the existence of "discipline problems" nor about whether or not I might have one. I hadn't any interest in the question of classroom control—I'm telling you how I felt about the matter then.

In order that learning may take place, Miss Bentley was saying, there must first be order. Mr. Grisson was nodding cordially. He was a man of perhaps fifty, gray-blond, going a bit bald. He spoke quietly but in quite definite and commanding tones like an actor or an officer. Miss Bentley was tall, solid and hard of limb, neat, and not unattractive; her age was perhaps thirty-five? It wasn't easy to tell. She didn't do much smiling. She had a job to do, she appeared to say, and if she seemed to look us over speculatively it was probably to wonder which of us was going to understand. Which would be able to help—who might hinder? It never occurred to her, I think, that someone might not choose to act the way she thought correct; if some of us didn't do so, it was because we couldn't understand. At least, that's the way I came to think later on in the year. At the time, I wasn't very interested.

Since that's a remark I've made twice now, I feel obliged to explain it. My lack of interest wasn't simply naïve, at least not in the way which springs immediately to mind, that of the imaginary progressive educator who imagines, or has been popularly supposed to imagine, that given a nice, friendly teacher and lots of freedom of action and very little planning, the students will always be good-natured, orderly, interested, motivated, well-behaved and studious, in short, nice themselves. I didn't doubt that there might be noise, disorder, anarchy, chaos and all that in my own classroom; I just didn't see that this constituted a "problem" any more than a quiet, studious class was a "problem." Perhaps they were both problems, put it that way. But what administrations mean when they say "problem" is something which is not supposed to happen, something which happens all the time of course, or it wouldn't be a "problem," but which isn't supposed to happen. A problem. You were supposed to believe in, and work toward, its non-existence.

Noise, quiet. I simply wasn't making any plans to promote one and forestall the other. I didn't feel I was going to do things, say things or try things with an eye to their result in terms of noise or quiet. I think I felt then, or would have felt had I thought about it, that you do what you want to do or can in a classroom, and then you see the result, or something of the result, and then you deal with that as you want to or can. One result isn't really much better than another, as far as you can tell. You don't know. I think that should be obvious to everyone by now.

What was I thinking about when I should have been interpreting the administration's careful clues? I remember thinking that I disagreed with Miss Bentley's one-way connection between order and learning. It was so obviously not necessarily so that I knew she couldn't mean it; it was just talk, something to say. (It wasn't; it was a clue.) I was a little surprised at myself and angry too, for thinking about it at all. For a year in the mountains near Yosemite I hadn't thought about what I agreed or disagreed with in terms of anything like "learning" or "education," and I frankly didn't plan to start now. To hell with all that. I remember being pleased though, that I was going to be working steadily, earning decent money and supporting my family. Then I remember thinking how pleased Fran would be about the job, and about the coming few free days before I went to work, how idly and pleasantly I meant to enjoy them.

(3) Welcome Back!

The first morning of the year at any school is bound to be pretty exciting and especially, it seems to me, at a junior high. You can stand around and watch the kids pour in, dressed as nicely as possible, all of them like yourself having forgotten momentarily what they're in for, yelling and laughing to each other, talking, asking questions—Whose room you got?—comparing summers and new shoes, all familiar and noisy and pleasant. Nothing is required of anyone so far.

I moved down through the kids to the end of the hall. There a huge new poster hung high on the wall above the stairs. WELCOME BACK! it said. Underneath these words a painted picture showed two kids, a boy and a girl, carrying lunch boxes and books, heading for school. An arrow sign painted in over on the side said

in case there was any doubt.

The only trouble with the poster was that these two life-sized painted kids didn't look like anybody I saw, or was likely to see, heading for old George Washington Junior High. The girl wore a blue sweater with buttons neatly painted down the front and a little round white collar on top; beneath that she wore a plaid skirt. The boy wore a white shirt, a red tie and a green letterman's sweater with a big W on it. They both wore brown-and-white saddle shoes.

The girl was a blonde. Her hair hung in a nice long curl around her shoulders. The boy had brown hair, combed straight back. They were both white. Not just Caucasian. The butcher paper on which they'd been painted hadn't been white enough to suit the artist or artists, and they had carefully painted the arms, legs, and faces of their subjects with a thick, shiny, white paint. They were the whitest kids I ever saw, and there they were, headed for the first day of school at George Washington Junior High.

(4) The Word

As I started up the stairs to my room, a man came around from the side out of the teachers' room and grabbed me by the arm.

Well, he said, how do you like it?

OK, I said cheerfully.

Let's see, I don't know all the new names yet. . . . You're Mr.—?

Herndon. Jim.

Glad to know you, he said. I'm the coach. We shook hands. Get to come to work without a tie. Best thing about the job.

Indeed, I could see he wore a sport shirt and windbreaker. He was a white man, perhaps forty-five, getting a little heavy.

Well, Jim, you can have it just two ways here, he said, keeping hold of my arm. Pretty good, or pretty goddam bad. Nothing in between. And it won't ever change either. However it starts for you, its gonna stay that way.

I waited. It was, again, just talk. He continued.

I've had some pretty good years here as a coach. You ever hear of————or————? He named two well-known Negro ballplayers. I had them both, one after the other, worked with both of them.

Listen, Jim, I always like to get in a word with the new men teachers. Like to help them start out right. The women, it's different. These ladies, especially these old colored ones, they have some kind of hold on the kids we don't. Jim, you ever work with these kids before?

No, I admitted.

I thought so. Well, now, the first thing is, you don't ever push 'em, and you don't expect too much. If you do, they'll blow sky-high and you'll have one hell of a time getting them down again. May never do it. Now, it's not their fault, we all know that. But you have to take them as they are, not as you and me would like them to be. That means, you find out what they can do, and you give it to them to do.

Now, that's true on the field just as much as in the classroom. Push 'em an inch more than that, and they blow. And you better find out real quick what they can do, otherwise you've lost them. Take on the field—I see a boy out there high-jumping and I might want to tell him, Look, boy, change your style of jumping to this or that way . . . I see something about how the kid's jumping, maybe. I see that if he changes, he'll get another two or three inches, maybe. Now, in a particular case that might just mean that he'd get on the track team here, or he might win the city meet, or it might mean—it depends on the case—he might make all-city. It might mean that when he gets down to the high school here he might be somebody. You ever stop to think how many kids from that high school make the big time in sports? How else are these kids going to make it?

But if I tell that kid that, change your style, chances are he might go crazy, yell and swear around, knock over the standards and throw out all the sawdust, get in everybody's way, ruin the whole period. I know that; I've seen it happen too many times. Not a one in a hundred that can take any kind of criticism. So, unless I know the boy well, I don't say anything. You see what I'm driving at?

The first bell rang then, and kids began to stream past us; they had five minutes to pull themselves together and find their classrooms. It saved me from having to answer. I was a little embarrassed; the guy was trying to help me out, and he was probably right. It sounded right then, and it sounds right now, as a description of how things were. It just didn't have anything to do with me. He was telling me how to keep out of trouble, but I couldn't see that I was in any, or was going to get in any. I wasn't making any plans, beyond going up to my room, taking the roll, and giving out the pencils. I moved to go up the stairs along with the kids.

Don't hurry, said the coach. You'll get there. This is important. Don't forget what I said. Now, the second thing is, The Word. You know about The Word yet?

He said it like that, in capitals, grinning at me. No, I said, chuckling. It seemed funny. What's The Word?

The Word is the one thing you can't ever let them say in the classroom. It's kind of a tradition around here, you might say. Any kid says The Word, then right down to the office with him, no arguing, ifs, ands or buts. Just make out the slip; all you have to write is The Word. They all know it, the kids, and they expect it. Now, this isn't an ordinary school in many ways, and one of the ways is swearing. You'll find you have to ignore a lot of talk you wouldn't dream of putting up with in some other place. My advice here is, forget it. It doesn't mean a thing, and if you try to stop it you won't get anywhere, and you won't have time to do anything else. But once they use The Word and you let them get away with it, they'll run all over you. Don't let 'em do it. Well—he grinned again—you know what The Word is now?

I laughed. Yeah, I said. I guess I do.

That's it, he said. That's the one. He looked around quickly though and whispered, just to make sure, *motherfucker*.

As I finally headed for class I thought I'd take his advice. It was something cut and dried, automatic, like taking the roll. If anyone said The Word I'd send them down, and that was that.

As it turned out, the only time The Word was ever spoken out loud in my class in its full glory was in such a bizarre context that I didn't do anything about it after all. Other than that once, it never came up. The kids all just said "mother," as in "you mother" or "look at that mother," and let it go at that.

No, that might be The Word as far as the teachers were concerned, but to the kids it made no difference at all.

So the only advice I was given which I felt like taking proved to be unnecessary. The Word didn't cause me no trouble. Unfortunately that didn't mean that there wasn't a word which did cause trouble, a word which, whenever it was spoken, caused an uproar, a violent argument, or a fight. If used in connection with someone not actually present in the classroom, it provoked the most immediate and unstoppable hilarity. Whooo-eee was heard from every side, the kids jumped up and down and sometimes fell down in the aisles pretending to be helpless with laughter. If spoken about, or to, someone present, the sound of the class was a lower and apprehensive Ooooooh? and there was trouble. The Word was *black*.

(5) *A to H*

The summer after I left the mountains I'd gone around applying for jobs on the basis of having my credentials, and in order to make that true I was obliged to take sixteen units of education work during the summer. You were only allowed to take nine, I discovered, but I took all sixteen anyway—nine at State, four at Berkeley, and three by correspondence. So if I was annoyed with myself, as I mentioned, for thinking at all about such things as even the most superficial theories of learning, it was probably because I'd had enough of it that summer. My plan was to go into the classroom and shut the door, leaving the rest of the school to run without my aid, suggestions or criticisms.

GW was already making that difficult. I might as well include here the type of thing that bothered me from the first. It was a kind of stubborn inconsistency between thought and action, stubborn because there seemed to be no reason for it. Since this is a real prejudice which I took with me into GW—which the school itself wasn't responsible for—it may perhaps have this chapter to itself.

I saw from my schedule that I taught five periods to four different groups—a seventh-grade B class, which I had twice, an eighth-grade B class, a ninth-grade D class, and a seventh-grade H class. Nothing had been mentioned in the meeting about a system of classification involving A's and B's, but inquiry around the coffee tables in the teachers' room had informed me that the kids were all rated A (high) to H (low) and placed in classrooms together accordingly. The ratings were made on the basis of IQ tests, standardized achievement tests, and, on occasion, faculty recommendation. Added to this imposing number of groups were a couple of classes which were supposed to be retarded and were naturally taught in the basement. I didn't know this detail until later on in the year, but I mention it now to complete the student body.

It is this kind of classification, based on this kind of testing, which seems to me the perfect example of the kind of thing that continually goes on in a school, and for which there is no reasonable explanation. Talking just to any teacher, as I did that year, you can hear a perfectly plausible lecture to the effect that IQ (or Mental Maturity, as it now goes) tests are not particularly valid under the best of conditions—that is, their validity is only general. You can't say, for example, that a child who scores 120 is any more capable than one who scores 116, 112, or anything above, say, 100. The Achievement Tests, which hope to measure what the child has actually learned in school, rather than what he may be capable of learning, have results equally hazardous of interpretation. If they tend to place a seventh-grade child at grade level 7.6, has that child actually learned more than the 7.1 or 6.9 child, and has he learned less than the 7.9 or the 8.2? Does one take tests well and another badly? Did one spend the sixth grade being drilled on punctuation and another writing science-fiction stories? Does one like to read? Was one ill when map-reading was going on? Did he have ringworm? Was he in Juvenile Hall? The questions are endless and also nonsensical, presenting you with a perfect (William) Jamesian confrontation but not, of course, much good for anything else.

Under the best of conditions, your teacher will say, not very valid. Not a description of much that is real, given any particular kid. You'll hear about something called "middle-class" values—that is, the tests are based on them—and that apparently means the middle-class kids can read and are used to following printed instructions. Even the "nonverbal" part of the test you have to read, since it's all still printed on paper, including of course the lengthy, repetitive and pretentious instructions. What about good old GW? Not so middle-class by a long shot, not to mention verbally adequate. Most teachers, I say, will give you that kind of talk, yet at the same time you'll probably find, in that teacher's grade book, alongside the names, the scores—116, 113, 118, 111, 115, like that—making it about a B class at GW. Come report-card time the teacher will be worrying about So-and-so whose IQ is at the bottom of her point spread and yet is doing A work. Like a gambler worrying about his own point spread when it doesn't work out, she may suspect a fix. In her class the 119's should be making A's, and the 111's should do C work. It's a comfort, I suppose, that surprisingly often these grade and IQ ratios worked out just right and no one had to worry about it.

The administration knows all of this too, of course. In fact, it is from the administrators that the teacher learns to disparage the scores. This may be the answer to the teacher part of the mystery. It is the kind of subject teachers quote administrators on, but rarely act upon unless forced to, because they know really that the administrator, whatever else he may be, isn't a teacher, doesn't give out grades, doesn't deal with thirty or forty kids at a time, so once you get in the classroom that administration talk doesn't count. What you need is something to back you up if you're in trouble, and perhaps the scores will do it.

But what about the administration, then? There are, of course, some quite good arguments for homogeneous grouping by ability, supposing you can get a valid way to discover this ability in the first place. (There are some equally good ones against any kind of ability grouping too, I should add.) It doesn't seem unreasonable, though, for an administrator, somewhat sophisticated about testing, to want to take his school population and divide it up into a couple of categories, calling them privately X and Y, or Giants, Yankees and Dodgers if he likes.

But for an administrator (knowledgeable and sophisticated) to administer these tests in large groups to the population of GW and from the results to carve himself out eight different ability groups, and to separate them in different classrooms and call them A to H, seemed to me incredible.

Consider the likely range of total scores involved. I'll place the cutoff point in IQ scores at 75. Below that and it's down in the basement. (This point varies; I seem to remember it was actually 79, but I can't be sure.) For the highs, let's say 135; there isn't any large group of students above that level in any school, and in any case it's not significant because the A group includes the greatest range of scores, being everything above a certain point.

So that at best you have a total of 60 points to be divided by eight, giving each division a range of 7½ points! In practice, given the much larger point spread of the A-group kids, the divisions included a smaller range of points—5½ to 6 points each.

But the administration has just been telling us at the faculty meeting—subject: testing—that 7½ points is meaningless in group testing as a standard by which to judge individual ability! The traveling psychologist is brought in from downtown to give us all the reasons I've mentioned and more besides. He's very convincing. A resource person from State adds his sociological piece about environment and social conditions, without mentioning, of course, The Word. (We teachers, black and white, stare into space and don't mention it either.) All right, so why the A to H, then? What the hell?

They were making it difficult, as I say. Had all these people said, Look, now, every IQ point counts and is significant, the 111 kid is exactly one point smarter than the 110 kid, and don't forget it, then the grouping would have made some sense, and I could have gone on in the room—and let the school run on and classify itself—without thinking about it. I suppose what I mean here is that I wasn't planning on coming into the school in order to disagree with the district or the administration on matters of policy and make a fuss about it. I wasn't interested enough in the district to do that. A nice, straightforward, lousy, wrong policy would have been fine with me.

Instead I kept wondering, so why the A to H? There didn't seem to be any kind of answer. No one asks the question, naturally. The lecture at the faculty meeting with the psychologist is one thing; running the school in real life is another. Both are valid, we all feel, but somehow the two just aren't connected.

There is no explanation either for odd events within the A-to-H scheme: why Virgil, who was in my H class, was one of the brightest kids I ever saw, or why John Banks, who couldn't read and might therefore be expected to have a little trouble with the tests, was in my B class and raising hell to boot. This is, of course, a different matter; however, since neither of them was around for very long, perhaps no one was required to give any answer.

(6) The Two B Classes

The coach was right. The first days really determined what I would be doing the rest of the year. Among other things it was made oddly clear that I would be spending relatively little of my time and energy on my two "best" classes, part of the elite of GW, my seventh- and eighth-grade B classes.

These two B groups were alike in a number of ways. They were of course alike in that they—the kids in them—had all scored within a few points of each other in the tests. But also, the individual kids within the groups looked alike—that is, the seventh-graders mostly looked as if they were about twelve years old and belonged in the seventh grade; they were about the same size, given the usual "big girls" and "immature boys"; they were normal, the big girls running everything and the little boys constantly in some kind of mild, disorganized trouble and wondering what those big girls were up to anyway. They were a class, recognizable as such. They acted like a class, they knew the routines of class; they came in and sat down, say, and waited to be asked to do something, talk, read, write, figure, answer questions, fill out forms on request, carry books, shut up. They might on occasion fail or refuse to do any or all of these things, but they expected them. They were with it.

Although my experience with the two B groups was completely different, this difference remained within the range of normal expectation. Briefly, the difference consisted in the fact that, whereas the seventh-graders were generally well-behaved, alert, somewhat studious, responsible, punctual, neat, got good grades and answered respectfully and politely, the eighth-graders were inattentive, resented assignments, did little unless threatened, whined about bad grades, never had pencils or notebooks or books, invented excuses to push themselves into an uproar, disliked school and teachers, me included, wised-off, were tardy, hypochondriacal before tests, and considered themselves picked on. If 7B was what all teachers call a good class, 8B was the prototype of bad.

Still, they were reasonable classes. If 8B was hard to deal with, you could think of reasons for it. Eighth-graders are a year older than seventh-graders—at that age, it means a lot. Seventh-graders are the youngest in the school and are apt to be fearful, polite and even ambitious. Eighth-graders, having learned the ropes, generally tend to be none of these. They are more interested in each other, having given up at least temporarily on the rest of the world, which they can see is adult and phony.

Beyond that, it's quite possible that these particular eighth-graders had crossed another borderline besides that of puberty —crossed over to where I was a white teacher and they were colored kids living in a Negro ghetto in a town full of Okies, restricted trade unions and middle-class liberal whites who lived in segregated neighborhoods on the tops of hills—a ghetto from which the roads out lead only to places like Chicago's South Side. However it was, and I don't really know how it was, my experience with 8B was bad from beginning to end. They remained for me a shallow, deceitful and uninteresting group who cordially disliked me and whom I grew to dislike in turn. 7B, on the other hand, I admired more and more. I had them twice a day, and looked forward to seeing them. Yet, it's true that although I liked and enjoyed them, they came to mean most importantly a respite, a breathing space, an armistice. That wasn't all they were, but it was mainly what they were.

It was simply that, on that first day, neither B class offered to become crucial enough, in the way that things at GW could become crucial. 8B was not bad or bored enough to worry me. I concentrated on keeping them in a semblance of order and schoolwork, and they concentrated on misbehaving and panicking just enough so there would be a minimum of order and schoolwork, but carefully short of getting themselves into any real trouble. None of them were real to me, with the exception of Ruth, whom I didn't consider as one of the class but just as Ruth. The class itself took advantage of her, not considering her as a member either but as someone who would do everything they were afraid to do, and using her actions as an excuse to laugh, yell, complain about unfairness and avoid assignments.

7B and 8B, all within five points of each other on the scores, one year apart, one good, one bad, both B. You won't read much more about them as groups—they'll only be mentioned, I imagine, from now on in terms of Ruth or John Banks or Opal Jameson, for the fact is that in terms of the school year and of this writing, they weren't matters of life or death.

It's not their fault; it's not mine either. Whose fault is it? For that answer I leave you to your *Time* magazines, your *Dissents,* your sociology texts, your NAACP's, your *Open Ends,* your Muslims, CORE's, Education Departments—to all your interpretations, whatever they are.

(7) Roll Call with 9D, 7H

9D and 7H were unreasonable. That first morning, finished with my nice seventh-graders and my second (free) period coffee, I climbed back upstairs. With the bell, 9D began to mosey into class. The excitement of the first day was all gone now; they remembered all about it and were already bored. Still everyone perked up as I began to call the roll; here was something everyone could do and at the same time impart a little individuality to his answer by intonation, hesitation or volume. I called off the names and everyone laughed at my pronunciation, the answering here's, yeah's and uh-huh's. We were all nervous. I went down the list.

Leon LaTour? I called out. No answer.

LaTour here? I tried again, pronouncing it like "sure."

Silence. I tried once more and a tall kid in the back got up. He stood for a moment looking at me. Finally he said, Tore.

What?

Tore. Leon LaTore. You ain't saying it right.

Oooooh? went the class. Why? I wondered. He hadn't done anything. Perhaps they knew he was just getting started. I waited, but nothing else happened. OK, LaTore, I said, and went on with the names.

After roll call, I wasn't quite sure what to do. I had nothing in particular planned, but had counted on the class to give me a hint, to indicate in some way what it was they wanted or expected. With 7B this had worked perfectly well. True, they had squabbled a little over the pencils and hadn't been able to restrain themselves from crowding around when books were passed out—as far as I could see, every student in the school suspected a permanent shortage of all materials—but they had soon settled down and pretty soon some kid asked what we were going to do, and we went on to talk reasonably about words like "social" and "society."

9D offered no clues. When I finished calling out the names, they waited passively for me to present them with some other challenge. Waiting for them to do the same, I busied myself at the desk with slips of paper, book cards, lists of names. 9D, seeing that I was leaving them alone, began to arrange themselves and get acquainted. They were fairly quiet, and, alphabetizing some cards, I actually forgot about them for a moment.

We had a long library table at the back of the room, in addition to the desk-chairs which stood bolted to the floor in rows. My own desk was in the front facing the rows, with a blackboard behind me and another on the wall to my left. The outside windows were to my right. I looked up and began watching the class. They were a sight. In the space of a few minutes they had forgotten that this was a class and that school was taking place. I had given them too a free gift, and they were making use of it. Perhaps they only pretended that this wasn't school, hopeful of keeping it up as long as possible until forced to do otherwise. However it was, they did it well; I felt oddly immobilized, and as if I shouldn't interfere. They were comfortable.

Most of the girls had taken out cosmetics, which they were applying. The boys were talking, laughing, mimicking the girls, showing off new jackets and shoes. Some kids were wandering around the room finding suitable places to spend the year. Three girls detached themselves from the group entirely and went back to sit at the long table where they had plenty of room to spread out purses, cosmetics, mirrors and combs. These were the three C's, as we all later called them, Charlene, Connie and

Cerise, and they were the prettiest and whitest girls in the class. Cerise especially had long, wavy (not curly) hair which hung around her shoulders, not blonde of course but brown anyway. The other two had shorter, but still soft and wavy, hair. They were light-colored; their lipstick and eye shadow showed up clearly. They sat at the table surrounded by tubes and jars and dared the boys to come over. The boys made plenty of smart remarks, but none came over then.

I kept watching the class. Remember how I said that, whatever else, the kids in 7B and 8B looked alike? Appeared to belong at least in the same room together? 9D hadn't this quality. At the time I would have conservatively estimated their ages to be anywhere from twelve or so (six small, extremely black little boys punching each other belligerently in the middle of the room) through eighteen or twenty (the three C's and a couple of other girls and Leon LaTore, for example) to about thirty. I say this extraordinary thirty because of another trio, Josephine, Geraldine, and May. They were three large, heavy *women,* big-breasted, medium-dark-skinned, hair plastered tight to their skulls, sitting stolidly and disapprovingly at the too-small desks as if planning never to arise. All three wore print dresses such as you imagine ladies wearing to picnics in Iowa. I expected them to start knitting something. I didn't know at the time what it was they disapproved of, but certainly if I had met them in, say, a bus station, I would have believed them to be thirty-year-old mothers of children and treated them accordingly. As a matter of fact, the records called all the kids in 9D fifteen years old, just as they should be, with the exception, as I recall, of one or two who were sixteen.

We didn't do anything else for the rest of the period. I didn't feel like interrupting them, and it was clear they were not going to give me a start. I thought I'd better try to figure them out; they had no unity that I could see, they were at loose ends . . . I had the sudden realization that I was going to be with them every day for about ten months. Near the end of the period I got up and announced that books would be given out tomorrow and we would start work. No one paid any attention, the bell rang, 9D wandered on out and I went down to lunch. I was not displeased with myself; I thought the day had gone pretty well. After lunch I had 7B again for English, then 8B and the no-trouble period with Ruth and, last period of all, I awaited 7H. I didn't have to wait long.

7H came charging and whooping up the stairs from where they had been studying mathematics with Mr. Brooks. Later I came to recognize their particular cries coming up my way. There's Roy, I'd think, there Harvey, there Vincent, Alexandra, picking their sounds out of the general outcry of the student body with a mixture of admiration and dread. 7H dashed in, flung themselves into seats and as quickly flung themselves out again. If 9D was willing to ignore me until doomsday, 7H didn't. They scattered from seat to seat, each trying to get as much free territory around him as possible, jumping up again as the area got overcrowded and ranging out to look for breathing space like Daniel Boone. From these seats, wherever they were, they confronted me with urgent and shouted questions, each kid, from his claim of several empty desks, demanding my complete attention to him: Are you a strict teacher? You going to make us write? When do we get to go home? Where our books? Our pencils? Paper? You going to give us them spellers? They were all finally outshouted by Roy, a boy about five feet six or seven inches tall with tremendous shoulders and arms, who stood in front of my desk, obscuring the view for all the rest, and just laughed as loud as he could for perhaps two minutes. Then he stopped and told everyone to shut up, because he knew this teacher wanted to take the roll. After some more shouting I finally did call it, listed the names of those absent on absence slips and clipped them to the wall over the door where a monitor from the office was to pick them up. I went back to my desk, wondered if I ought to pass out pencils (I'd learned something), thought a bit about books, and decided to give out some spellers.

At that moment there came a tremendous outcry from over by the door. I looked over and three or four kids were standing there, looking up at the door and yelling their heads off.

Naturally the rest of the class soon began shouting insults at them, without any idea of what the trouble was. Everyone was standing up; calls of "watermelon-head!" filled the room. The kids by the door wheeled and rushed up to me, furious and indignant. Vincent, who was one of them, was crying. What the hell? I began to yell in turn for everyone to shut up, which they soon did, not from the effect of my order but out of a desire to find out what was the matter; they sat back to hear the story. The four were Roy, Harvey, Vincent and Alexandra, and what they demanded to know was why had I put their names up there on those absence slips? They weren't absent! Was I trying to get them into trouble? We here, Mr. Hern-don! They didn't want to get in no trouble! Alexandra began to threaten me with her mama. Roy, tempted beyond his own indignation, began to make remarks about the color and hair quality of Alexandra's mama. It shows how upset Alexandra was; it was fatal to ever mention your mother at GW, which Alexandra of all kids knew quite well.

For a moment I thought maybe I had put the wrong names up by mistake, but I checked them and saw that wasn't so. I displayed the slips, spread out on my desk. Their names weren't there. The names on those slips were not theirs, I told them. Right? They weren't satisfied. They demanded a closer look at them slips. I handed the slips around, whereupon it became a scene out of some old movie when Stepin Fetchit turns the letter upside down and sideways before giving it to Bob Hope to read, explaining he doesn't read Chinese. The fact was, Harvey, Roy, Vincent and Alexandra were having a little trouble reading their own names.

Finally Alexandra let out a screech and started for the back of the room, where a little tiny kid, black and scrawny, jumped smoothly out of her way, grinning at her, holding onto a desk in front of him ready to jump again. Alexandra was demanding something from him; she was joined by Roy *et al;* and I finally made out that they were calling on him to verify my statement about their names and the slips. He wasn't doing that, apparently, so they all rushed back to me. All four now shouted that

Virgil had told them their names were up there on them slips and they were getting into trouble for cutting school. The first day! The class began to hoot all over again. I started for Virgil, who left his chair and sped over by the windows.

I sped after him. Whooo-eee! Everything was great! Right away I saw I wasn't about to catch Virgil—I'd had some idea about making him recant in public—and stopped. Virgil promptly dashed out the door.

Just about then the monitor came along for the slips and I collected them and handed them over. The four kids still stood there. Were they in trouble or weren't they? They didn't know for sure, but probably they did know what they were up against here all of a sudden, just as I suddenly knew what I was going to be up against. As the monitor was leaving, a water bomb made from a folded sheet of school paper came flying through the open transom and exploded on the floor in the front of the room.

After school I hurried out to the nearest bar to have a beer and think it over. Things weren't the same as they had been this morning, or even at noon. There was Roy, a broad-shouldered, thick-chested *man* of thirteen, largely out of control, probably stronger than I. Vincent, a little kid, worried, thin, wore a sports coat and a tie for the first day of school. Harvey looked like a country boy, wearing jeans, a light jacket, high work shoes; it wasn't just his clothes, though, it was the way he walked—steady, serious, trying to puzzle it out, willing to, but no go. Alexandra—dark, handsome, proud, mean, bitter, able to whip any boy in the class except Roy—in looks and temperament a gypsy.

Their situation was simply that they couldn't read their own names when I wrote them on the slips. So that when Virgil told them I'd turned them in, they didn't have any way at all to find out if it was true or not. They had to believe it, at first anyway. They knew, somehow, that Virgil could read, and that was all the certainty they had to go on. Next they could ask me. Could I be trusted? After all, Virgil just told them I was trying to get them into trouble (and Virgil could read) and so it was only logical that I would lie about it. If Virgil was right, I couldn't be believed. But what about Virgil? There they were again, back to the simple fact that they couldn't tell their own names from anyone else's, and this was to be their situation every day and every period of the year.

But what about Virgil? Here was a kid who was not only mean enough but smart enough to figure out this foolproof method of driving four other kids nuts on the very first day of school, and who was also prepared in advance—for he hadn't had time to construct it out there in the hall—with a water bomb to throw in through the transom when he ran out . . . when I chased him out, as he said the next day by way of excusing his illegal departure.

I couldn't help it. I went down the next day before class and looked up old Virgil's IQ. It happened to be, at last testing, 138. I was going to ask one of the counselors just what he was doing in group H, but while I waited for them to show up I read farther down the card. After a lot of written comments like "troublemaker" and "adjustment difficulty to classroom situation" and a couple of referral dates to Juvenile Hall, I found the letter H, followed by the words *Teacher Recommendation.*

(8) Apologia

A few words for 7B. I've already said that they were attentive
and responsible, but they were a lot more than that. With them
I was able to make a start toward working things out for myself,
what I actually wanted to teach, how to do it, how to approach
things in a way that might mean something to all of us. For
instance, whatever I read during this time, the fall of the year,
seemed to lead me into some idea for the classroom and I would
come charging in with the idea, usually half-baked, to try it out
on them. They would respond as enthusiastically as they could,
sometimes while utterly confused, often just humoring me
awhile and passing out subtle hints for me to come to my
senses. But with them the pressure was always off—I was free
and easy. In effect, they allowed me to teach myself.

I often wondered how they got along outside my classroom.
In the world of and around GW, most of the kids were scared—
scared of failure, scared of being black, scared of their new
shoes, scared of tearing their clothes, scared of not knowing
how to do right, scared of not getting a pencil or a piece of three-
hole lined paper upon which they would be too scared to write
anything much if they got it. Perhaps the students of 7B fell
back, outside the classroom, as individuals, into this scariness
and became apathetic or violent or ugly, or called each other

watermelon-head. I really don't know. It seemed as if in the classroom they had found something reasonable to respond to, as often an individual kid will find in school some promise which is kept, something sensible or even beautiful, something not available in their homes or families or on their blocks, and so come to live really only at school, even sometimes to love it and find in it the same joy and despair as any lover.

Perhaps that's too much said. The kids of 7B, by and large, found solidarity in their classroom; they had it, they accepted it. They were also, without any question, my solidarity. In this connection I'd like to mention the names of Ramona Williams and Hazel Lopez, the unofficial and real leaders of 7B and examples to their classmates; they were two of the loveliest little girls I've ever known, and I could always count on them.

(9) Maurice

I determined to pass out English books and spellers to 9D, to make everything official, and get down to work. The main work, I'd decided, was going to be composition, freely done and at length. With a lot of written material on hand, theirs—in which, having written it themselves, they were bound to be interested— we could later get down to making some corrections, show up some common faults, use the books to find practical standards for usage and punctuation. The spellers I'd use for regularity; they weren't much good, being just lists of words and a number of rather silly things to do with those words, but I thought we'd do them anyway, half the period twice a week perhaps. They were simple enough and it would be a kind of breather for everybody.

9D, however, having received the free gift, wasn't about to let go of it as easy as that. It's true they scrambled around for the books and spellers, but they quickly withdrew into a more dignified aloofness as soon as it became clear there were enough to go around, which was only when every single person had one of each. Cosmetics came out, kids got up and began searching for new places to sit, a boy took out a transistor radio, the C's withdrew to the back table. I passed out paper; I began to talk about what we were going to do. Cosmetics and conversation continued—not loudly or aggressively, but just as if I weren't addressing them. I began to insist on everyone's attention. Perhaps ten kids had their backs to me by now. I called kids by name, requiring their attention. They began to resent it. Finally a voice said, Teacher, why don't you let us alone?

That stopped it. Ooooooh? they all went. The speaker was Verna, a tall, lanky girl, brown, lithe and strong-looking, plain-faced, kinky-haired, without makeup. She was making a stand. The tone of the class implied apprehension and excitement: I was now going to throw Verna out. Actually I didn't give a damn. Verna and I had everyone's attention; the others had momentarily lost. Verna had to say something, if only to get the last word before being thrown out. I expected an outburst, but instead she said, You should have made us get to work yesterday. All the other teachers made us get to work. If you want us to do work, why didn't you make us yesterday?

She stopped talking and immediately turned around, her back toward me. The class rallied to her support by taking up their conversations where they had left off. Now I was losing. I got ready to start insisting again, wondering what I was going to say if and when they started listening.

Then the door swung open, and a kid walked in, came over and handed me a slip and found a seat near the back of the room. The class turned around and conversed in a different key. The subject was the newcomer, Maurice, particularly the fact that he had just gotten out of Juvenile Hall in time to make the second day of school. Teacher, Maurice just back from Juvi! shouted out somebody, so I didn't have any trouble finding out. Maurice himself was subdued and quiet, having been warned, I suppose, to be nice or find himself right back in Juvi. But I was winning again; they were so curious about what I was going to say to Maurice about Juvi that they had to recognize me, just to make sure I knew about it. I passed a book and a speller down the row to Maurice. You supposed to report to the parole officer about Maurice, teacher! How he do, if he do his work! Do he get in trouble or fighting! . . . I began to get advice from all sides.

Well, now, I said, actually this is not a class about Juvi, but about English. Whooo-eee! That broke them up. But when they stopped laughing they were attentive enough. I began to talk about how English meant using the language however they wanted; I was well into my speech about figuring out together what was relatively interesting to do and then figuring out how to do it—which was, naturally, crap since I already had the business of composition in mind and how we were going to go about it—and they were just beginning to get bored (they knew it was crap too), seeing as how I wasn't going to either lecture Maurice about Crime Not Paying or say anything humorous again, when *bang!* Maurice and another boy, locked in each other's arms, fell over their desks and across the desks of the next row and lay there stretched out, struggling. Books, papers and kids scattered. Hell!

Whoooo-eee! I got over there. Silence. Let go! Both of you! I shouted, but nothing happened. Maurice was on top, the other kid across a desk, and as I got there Maurice loosed an arm and belted the other kid in the face. Cut it out! I grabbed Maurice. He didn't come. The kid on the bottom let go, but Maurice didn't. I tugged him rather gently. He belted the kid again. I got mad, grabbed Maurice under the arms and heaved as hard as I could. Maurice flew backward over the row of desks and landed with a crash on the next row. He landed plenty hard; I imagine it hurt, and also he must have thought it was all up with him, back to Juvi. He was frantic and mad. He jumped up and started for me. I stood there; he stopped and stood there. He glared. Everybody was scared. No one in the class looked forward, suddenly, to what was going to happen, which was that Maurice was going to come for me and hit me or I him; the end would be the speedy return of Maurice to Juvenile Hall, beaten up by me previously or not. It was inevitable.

We stood there quite a few seconds and then I nodded, turned and walked swiftly back to my desk and sat down. I hoped I was implying a mutual cease-fire among equals. When I turned around toward the class, Maurice had likewise retreated and was sitting at his desk. We carefully didn't look right at

each other, but still in the same general direction, so as not to
be accused of avoiding anything either. Maurice had seen the
issue—I'd say we saw it exactly alike. We both had something
at stake, and he cooperated perfectly. It was like a play, or an
improvisation which came off just right. We were winning.

The class was dumbfounded. They waited, disappointed but
certainly somewhat relieved. Students at GW courted disaster;
that doesn't mean they liked it. They didn't believe the action
was over. They knew better. So they were all attention when I
got ready to say something—considering the last thing I'd said
about Juvi, they had high hopes. Instead I said, All right, I
guess we can start classwork. The first English assignment is to
write a story about what just happened. You can begin writing
now, finish it tonight, and have it ready for tomorrow's class.

Whatever they'd expected, that wasn't it. It suddenly seemed
like a lousy idea to me, and I decided to admit it and do
something else, but before I could Verna said Shhh! loudly and
turned around in her seat so her back was to me. The class
woke up at that signal and began to yell demands and questions
at me. All of a sudden they were just like 7H.

What to write! How we spozed to write without no paper!
That ain't no schoolwork, teacher! You can't make us write
about that! I ain't got no pencil! You trying to get us into
trouble! No pen! No paper! What to write! What to do!

Panic. Instead of the moral lecture they expected to enjoy
from an indignant teacher, here I was making them supply the
lecture themselves. Everything was going wrong. Quiet! I yelled
a few times. That was more like it, and everyone subsided.
Thirty-year-old May raised her hand placidly. I called on her
gratefully, but she said, Teacher, why don't we do our spellers?
I got furious at once. Spellers? I was proposing to write
seriously about this exciting event and she wanted instead to put
a silly list of words in alphabetical order or backward according
to last letter, or whatever it was for Unit 1 in the goddam
speller! You teaching this class or am I? I snapped at her.
Whoooo-eee! He sure cut down old May! By now I was determined on the assignment again.

What's the problem? I asked the class. Things happened in here today. All I'm asking you to do is to write about it. Why don't you get started?

What to write? everyone started asking again. Quiet! I shouted at once. A series of sarcastic questions tempted me. You were here, weren't you? Right? You have eyes? Right? You all have ears? OK. Now think about what happened in this same room, describe it, tell it to yourself, remember it, and then write it down. Never mind the spelling for now, never mind ink, just write it down however you can. That's all!

Shhh—loudly again. This time not from Verna, but from Leon LaTore in the back. No one ever said *shit* at GW, only *shhh!* or, to express extreme disgust, *sheee!* Shhh! said Leon LaTore, nobody going to write that. He was addressing the class, not me. He just want to pin it on somebody. He want to find out about it. He want to pull you in on it!

Twenty-five protestations of innocence and as many accusations and counter-accusations followed that. Finally people's mamas began to be mentioned, and I had to yell Quiet! again. Well, what if I do want to know? I yelled. Do you know? Something started it, didn't it? Here's Maurice pounding on somebody, on Fletcher there, all of a sudden. Do you think he wanted to? So who did start it, then?

Accusations, etc. Leon LaTore grinned in the back. Finally Verna jumped up and yelled, Hush up, you-all! Sit down, big-leg! came an unidentified voice. Forget you! said Verna coldly, and everybody hushed. You don't have to get all shook up, said Verna. She was talking to me. Everybody know who start it. Robert he took hold of Maurice's notebook while Maurice writing on them cards you give him for the books, and slip it over onto Fletcher's desk, and Maurice look up and find it gone and then he see it on Fletcher's desk and grab it, but Fletcher don't know it Maurice's because he didn't see that Robert put it there so he grab it back and there they go.

No one denied it. Robert was out of his seat and backed up in the corner of the room like John Dillinger facing the FBI. He looked like an authentic fourteen-year-old, small, stocky, black.

Sit down, Robert, I said. Oooooh? went the class softly. Shhh!
said Leon LaTore. Verna wasn't convinced. Ain't you sendin'
Robert to the office, teacher? she said flatly.

I was tired of the whole thing. Property. Your mama. It
seemed likely that at the moment Robert was slipping Maurice's
notebook over, every other kid in the class was grabbing,
poking, pushing or pulling at some piece of someone else's stuff.
I told them so. Robert waited warily in the corner. Sit down,
Robert, I said again. I looked at the clock; there were only
about five minutes left. OK, I said, now go on and write the
assignment, now we all know all about it.

Actually no one wrote the assignment; no one, that is, except
for Maurice, who perhaps figured he'd better. No one remembered it the next day; all denied any knowledge of its being
assigned. I read Maurice's "Compostion," as it was entitled: A
boy took another boy('s) (notebook) in the class and so the
boy jump(ed) him to beat (him) the teacher broke it up But
the teacher didn't send the boys to the office.

(Corrections mine.)

(10) Another Apology

This apology, which is to the reader, is for the end of violence. One kid flipped over the desks, a brief facing-up, that was all. No switchblades, zip guns, chains, brass knuckles, razors. It would have been interesting and fun to write about myself as a kind of sheriff-teacher continually fighting it out with outlaw-students—*Pow!* Got him! Take that! etc.—and as a matter of fact it might have made working at GW rather exciting. I don't mind a bit of violence myself, and many's the fantasy I had that year, lying awake at night, in which I let Leon LaTore or John Banks or Roy (or their mamas) have it right in the mouth!

The only other incident was a little slugging—which, unfortunately for everyone, didn't involve the students but myself. That is, it involved the student only as object, and I would have given a lot right then to take it back. So much for the relationship of fantasy to George Washington Junior High. I'm not even eager to write about it, but then it doesn't come up for quite a few pages.

But outside of that, no more violence for me, not even come springtime. You have to remember that these students are really children—seventh grade to ninth grade, ages twelve to thirteen, thirteen to fourteen, and fourteen to fifteen, all this talk about eighteen-year-olds and thirty-year-olds notwithstanding. Maybe they had switchblades and zip guns somewhere, but they weren't in evidence in my classes. Obviously 7B didn't need them. 8B was too chicken. 7H and 9D were the only real possibilities for that kind of action, but there we didn't have the time for it. From the very start we were too busy being intellectuals.

(11) .025, or 97½ percent

Ninety-eight percent Negro was how GW was described downtown. One day I figured out how I stood. I had 35 kids in 7B, 32 in 8B, 28 in 9D and 26 in 7H. In the latter two I never had a full class or even close to it—they were gone, somewhere, just not present. Occasionally I would be notified that So-and-so wouldn't be showing up for ten days or two weeks, and often the kids could tell me what happened. Juvi, moved, went to live with So-and-so, ringworm, had to baby-sit. In any case, taking the registered number, which was what the downtown average was based upon, I had all together 121 students. Of these all but two were Negro.

The two weren't white exactly; they were Japanese. No one knew what to make of the Oriental students at GW; were they white or black? Neither? Then what to do? Being neither one, you were simply out of it and didn't count, no matter what the downtown figures said. My two weren't outstanding—the thing is, they were both in 8B, which bothered me in my percentages. Didn't that make 8B high on the non-Negro side proportionally? And aren't the rest of them 100-percent black?

Well, I consigned them to a general margin for chance along with my other non-Negro who came along later in the year. Counting her, that made three out of 121, for a percentage of .025 white or not Negro, and 97½ percent colored, Negro or black. I had to admit that made me about even and there was no discrimination in evidence.

(12) Luck

I've already said that the first days established everything. I've said that between 8B and me there existed no real relationship—we were just getting through the year. I've implied that between 9D and 7H and me there was, or was going to be, something going on. I've mentioned Maurice and John Banks.

When Maurice and I acted out our parts that day, I was established in a certain way, part, role. No doubt I could have changed it, but I didn't want to. What was established was that whatever went on in the class was to be kept to ourselves, that I wasn't sending them to the office or writing notes about them to the counselors if they messed up. During the year, in fact, I did send plenty of them to the office, but I didn't send them, and they knew I wouldn't send them, for anything serious or crucial. I sent them for chewing gum or not staying in their seats—when I was mad or irritated or had just had enough of them, sometimes for very little reason at all—and of course very little happened to them in consequence. I was satisfied with the part because it was the only way I could ever know what they really would do in class themselves, wanted to do, desired. It seemed to me that any kind of halfway measure or bargaining would be useless with them. Either you weren't going to threaten them or you were going to, and if you did then you could never tell at all how they really felt; they would always be reacting (which is different) to what I thought, wanted, as they saw it. At the time I thought that was very important.

About a week after school opened, John Banks entered 8B. He came in without any notice or pass or excuse, no sign of official recognition. He entered the room after everyone else had sat down, walked around, spoke a word here and there, patted some girls and drew from them shrieks and giggles. I decided to get a little recognition myself and asked his name. John. More wandering, past my desk; I risked another inquiry. Could I see his slip from the attendance office? No comment. John Banks crazy as hell, teacher! came Ruth's voice from her seat. You come near me, John Banks, I'll hit you with this chair! John Banks didn't swerve, stop or notice, just breezed past Ruth and only his hand came up to slide, wave, casually past her face. Now what? Nothing was going to happen in class until this was settled, I could see that, so on the next go-round, I stepped in front of him. He took no notice, only moved with the same careless stroll as if to just go around me, an obstacle, a desk perhaps, which happened to get in the way. He didn't feel like moving the desk, me, out of the way at the moment. He was an ordinary-looking kid, not tall or short, slim, brown, strong-looking. John Banks cold! said someone admiringly from the class. As he moved around me I put out an arm. Wait a second, I said, you're supposed to have an admit slip—he moved back to go around the other way—telling me you belong in this class. He was slipping past when I stuck out the other arm. Hold it, I said again. He never stayed still, dodging slowly around the other way again, his eyes moving past mine, looking at nothing at any time, saying I have to hold it, you in the way. What was the class doing all this time? Watching.

Banks! I said sharply. Make up your mind: either get in a chair or get out! I was pretty scared of him. Later on I could remember that he was only a fourteen-year-old kid after all, but unfortunately I remained scared of him. Well, he did sit down, more or less falling back into a desk. His hands and eyes continued to wander. When I asked him for his pass, he poked the kids in front and around him, not hard or violently, but just a touch on the shoulder of one, an easy shove on the neck of another, while the kid behind him found his pencil rolling off the desk. These kids all made outcry. I gave up on him, as I had to. He'd made the one concession he was going to make in sitting down, but he didn't figure he had to answer me or write on the book cards I gave him or even accept the books, which somehow fell off onto the floor. Pick them up, please! He picked them up, and they mysteriously slid off again. Outcries from surrounding kids, and from Ruth on the other side of the room: John Banks stay in this class I have to kill him! We went on with whatever lesson it was, but not really. Not even 8B's usual pretense of academic eagerness was present. Everyone watched John Banks out of the corner of his eye—no one followed instructions or knew the place or heard his own name when called. When the class left at the bell, John Banks's books remained behind on the floor.

So the next day when 8B came in and John Banks repeated the performance, wandering, ordered to sit, sitting, poking, etc., I wrote out a slip, said OK, John, and sent him to the office. He left the room without comment.

He won't go to the office, teacher, shouted the kids. They were disgusted with me. You spozed to send some other kid down there with that slip and then after the other kid get back, then you send John Banks! But that advice got argument too. Who going with the slip, bigmouth? said someone. It became clear that no one wanted to take a slip down on John Banks. They argued about it awhile.

He went though. In about fifteen minutes back he came, escorted by Miss Bentley. The class fell silent. She was a changed woman; stiff, cold, commanding, indescribably mean-looking. We all felt guilty; it was our fault that John Banks was misbehaving—that was her word for what John Banks had been doing.

John has been misbehaving in class, he tells me, she said, looking around the room. He has promised to behave and to waste no more of your time, Mr. Herndon's time, or his own time. Sit down, John, she added, and he walked up a row toward the back of the room. As he got there, he began to recover a bit, began to saunter, reached out a hand for a girl's hair, grinned. John, said Miss Bentley sharply, where is your seat? He shrugged. I ain't got no particular seat in this class, Miss Bentley, he said. She glanced at me. Now I was guilty. Take the third seat in row five. Right there. She pointed. John went over to it and sat down. She looked over the class again, looked at me, and left.

Well, I only bring up John Banks to show that it was probably just luck that established the relationships and roles in my classes; the difference between one class and another, between something happening and nothing happening, may turn out to be simply the difference between John Banks and Maurice. At GW you are more likely to get John Banks than Maurice. Not that many kids are in the same shape as John Banks under ordinary circumstances, but given the kind of thing that happened to Maurice only a few hours after coming out of Juvenile Hall, I think 90 percent of the kids at GW would have acted in some way like John. Why not Maurice? I don't know; he wanted badly enough to get through the day, the year perhaps, and had brains enough to see how to do it. John Banks didn't want that or, like most of the kids there, didn't believe in it and was settling for something else more immediate or possible.

It was Ruth, by the way, who told me he couldn't read or write, and later, in a meeting about him with counselors and other teachers, it turned out to be true. Anyway, his behavior, as they say, didn't improve or change. Miss Bentley informed me, when I asked her about it later, that John Banks was difficult to handle unless you were firm. So I would be firm and get him in his seat, and then I'd have to be firm again and get him to stop poking So-and-so and then firm some more to get him to pick up his books; I could see that I was going to have to spend all period every day doing nothing but being firm with John Banks, so I gave up on him, let him alone until things got too bad, and then got firm or sent him out. He was apparently going to stay there in 8B, and he was out of my league.

John Banks cold! That was about all anyone would ever say about him. Maurice's case, in contrast, was discussed up one side and down the other by almost everyone; who was right, who wrong, what I should have done, what they would have done in either position—and with that as precedent, the cause and motive and rationale of every incident was discussed in 9D right from the start, predictions of other possibilities made and theorized about; they were intellectuals all of a sudden.

But with John there wasn't anything to talk about. Once a kid in 8B did say to me that it was too bad I happened to get John in my class. You know, teacher, you didn't have to have John Banks you might make out all right. John Banks cold!

Skates was the only one who had any explanation for John Banks's continued stay in the B group. Miss Bentley made him a bargain, he said. She's told him he can stay in the B group as long as he behaves himself, as long as he doesn't kill anybody or burn the school down. That's how she can control him—she just threatens him with the basement, where he thinks he belongs. Hell, that's the whole story. Skates, however, was full of a number of wild tales.

(13) Skates

Skates's classroom was right next to mine—the only one, since mine was at the end of the building—and also he was the only teacher who lived near me. We arranged to ride to work together, taking turns driving.

Skates was a big young guy, twenty-six or so, from Chicago, and if there was anything he really hated it was teaching school. This goddam lousy job! he would shout a hundred times daily. He used to talk a lot about being the youngest son of a Jewish family, explaining to me what all that meant; the older brother was making a lot of money in Chicago selling discount rugs and so someone in the family had to start at the other end and be professional. Professional, don't make me laugh! he'd howl, but his old parents were happy; they had everything now, lots of dough and a professional son besides. The only good thing about the teaching business, according to Skates, was the Federated Teachers of America, the teachers' union (AFL–CIO), for at least with the FTA all you had to do was to be a lousy, stinking teacher in a lousy, stinking job. You didn't have to go on and be a dirty, finking, scabbing, bootlicking, son-of-a-bitch lackey of the reactionary, murdering administration or the petty-bourgeois parents and their phony, rude kids.

Skates said that in Chicago the union was the terror of

administrators, superintendents and boards of education. There was none of this crap about three-hour teachers' meetings, yard duty, extra jobs like collecting money for pictures or yearbooks and so on. They want to have a meeting in Chicago, it's fine! he'd say. Pay overtime! When it costs them, they pretty soon see how important the goddam meetings really are! In Chicago, apparently, you got paid overtime every time you turned around, you accepted no student beyond your maximum class load, the principal didn't say, Come on down to my office on your free period, he asked you if you could find it convenient to drop by anytime, and so on. It was paradise. Influenced perhaps by this, even if I wouldn't say I actually believed it all, I joined the FTA about the end of September. Skates was the leader of the GW unit, then there was myself and one other man, a plump, middle-aged Irishman. The Irishman wasn't a bad guy, although he was full of talk about political connections in town and liked jokes about sex and colored folk; I thought he was being noble at first to take on the Reading Improvement class when it was started about this time, but it turned out that the class size was limited to fifteen and he could kick out any kids who gave him trouble. Anyway the Irishman also belonged to the CTA (the California Teachers Association), which Skates called a lousy, stinking company union, and almost every other organization in the city. Later on in the year two other new teachers joined us, both young Negro guys who were having their troubles on the job and hoped the union would go to bat for them. We didn't have meetings ourselves, for anything Skates wanted to say to us he could just come around and tell us.

Our rides to and from school were full of blast and outrage. Skates was permanently furious at almost all the normal conditions of life. Not only the school situation, which he called feudalism, but his car—he should have known better than to buy what he called a lousy Kraut Volkswagen!—his apartment and landlady, and most of all his lousy social life in this lousy city. His chief gripe was the lack of beautiful women willing to sleep with him, despite his many trips to the hotel tea dances, the hundreds of martinis he paid for and the numerous girls he persuaded to enter his lousy Kraut car, and despite also the lousy members of the lousy Jewish community whom he expected to furnish a supply of willing females. There were a few, he admitted, but Skates wanted nothing less than 100-percent success. We discussed the details of his amours almost every morning.

He was, oddly enough, outraged at the local Negro community for not offering him the kind of relaxation he was used to in Chicago. Where's the whores? he wanted to know. Where's all the swinging clubs? Where are the goddam jitney girls? What the hell good was it to have the kind of Negro ghetto that was inevitable under capitalism if there weren't even any jitney girls? Who did those spades think they were? Did they think they were living under socialism?

All this would be punctuated, if he was driving, with the most outlandish curses at other drivers who happened to turn or change lanes or stop at stop signs or do anything at all, legal or illegal, that forced Skates to turn the steering wheel or touch the brake. He wanted to go in a straight line at a constant speed without stopping at all, and nothing short of that would do. Those drivers should all be killed! He would shove them into death camps! Can't you drive, you f——— Cossack, you! he'd yell out the open window to a startled driver. I was always expecting men to stop their cars and beat hell out of both of us, but Skates never worried about it. Let 'em get out of their goddam bloodsucking cars, he screamed. I'll run right over 'em! They'll never know what hit 'em! I'll smash you, you criminal, he yelled to another passing car, you lousy, peasant-murdering bastard!

I was intrigued by the idea of the jitney girls, who apparently drove up and down the streets of the South Side in Chicago in oversized cars, picking up men who flagged them down for a quick one. I was even more interested in Skates's combination of a kind of exaggerated, almost comic Stalinism (it's the only word that applies, old-fashioned as it sounds) and his open contempt for what he must have referred to at one time as our colored comrades as exemplified by that same Negro community and the students of GW. He railed at the kids in class in the same way, to their great delight; occasionally passing his room on my way to coffee, I could hear him calling them Cossacks and finks and yelling they'd better learn to tap-dance, they certainly weren't learning anything else. From the first, Roy called him The Crazy Teacher.

(14) The Tribe

Skates called our students The Tribe. Watch out today, he'd yell to me coming down the hall for lunch, The Tribe's getting edgy! Or, Come into my room, The Tribe's holding a talent show, tap-dancing, strippers, the whole bit! It's a little gift from me, in appreciation they didn't eat me up last week!

Through October I seemed to spend my time talking to everyone, other teachers, students—D's and H's particularly, I guess—in an effort to discover . . . what? Where we were, what everyone wanted, needed, a kind of late orientation to GW. The hot weather was past, the World Series over with, the holiday season in view. What I began to see was a set of characteristics of The Tribe: characteristics which, indeed, I began to think were rather clear-cut and few in number. Many things which might have seemed definitive ended up not being so; they were traits shared by others, elsewhere, not only of The Tribe, or else they weren't important to The Tribe.

Language is an example. Excluding the use of various common epithets applied to Negroes in America, their language and accent was all just more or less Southern, ranging all the way from the "reckoning" and "commencing" kind of talk to just "ah" instead of "I" or "er." They didn't care for the "s" of the third person singular, and accentuated this by rarely using auxiliaries, so that you heard, He a good man, He fight all the time, She trying to get me in trouble. Even when they were reading aloud from a text, nothing would convince them that that "s" at the end of a verb was in decency pronounceable. But many Americans, I think, are attracted to Southernisms; almost all popular singers use some variation of a Southern accent (witness even such old, inappropriate guys as Woody Herman) so that where there were many more common outrages against proper usage than those mentioned, it very soon began to cease to matter. My own ear soon heard it as normal and my own tongue came to utter it too in the end.

Poverty was not crucial either, at least not in the sense of not having food, clothing and shelter. The Tribe didn't live in a slum. A ghetto, yes, but driving people through the area, as a friend of mine used to do, failed always to shock them considerably or stir them to any powerful social consciousness. What they saw was rows of houses, not apartment buildings, with yards, mostly wooden or stucco houses, some well-kept up, some badly kept up, some painted, some not. No one would have thought it a rich neighborhood, but neither did one automatically think of rats, garbage and TB either. The rents, I should mention, were extremely high, which made it necessary for two or three families to share these ordinary-looking houses in many cases; this known, the aspect of the district is changed. Still, the kids had money in their pockets for the school snack-bar food—you could tell who had more and who had less money by whether they were eating hamburgers or a large plate of mashed potatoes and gravy; these items were the same price, but whereas the hamburger tasted better (and besides was what you were spozed to eat in America), one of them didn't fill you up, you had to have two. They also had candy, gum, potato chips, all that kind of stuff; they had records and phonographs and could bring them to school; they had tennis shoes and gym clothes, basketballs, bicycles, cigarettes, cosmetics aplenty, and Japanese transistor radios. All of this wasn't scot-free; some of these things weren't problems, but some were.

Fathers were not a thing commonly possessed by members of

The Tribe, but even that's not so outright as it might appear. I know it's a platitude about what all the interpretations call the matriarchal Negro society or culture. For one thing, its not unique in that respect, and for another I'm not certain how much difference it makes. The district had figures to show that about 85 percent of the families of GW were fatherless. However, these figures were presented to us at a teachers' meeting after school which was presided over by someone from the Welfare Department downtown, and it was also from the Welfare that the figures came. I remember little about the meeting itself except that the teachers joined the Welfare in expressing their outrage about all the county welfare money going to support certain undeserving people from Arizona, Texas or wherever, all of whom only came to California and specifically this very city because they knew the welfare rates were high. My own outrage came from the fact that the meeting lasted until almost six o'clock. The point is, families don't get much welfare money if there is some big, able-bodied dad around the place, so that it's just possible that out of all those officially fatherless families there may have been a few who just neglected to mention Dad at all, or forgot to report that he was out to sea or working in San Pedro or somewhere, coming home only weekends like quite a number of dads anywhere you go. With rents as high as they were, jobs scarce and layoffs frequent, no one was going to miss out on that welfare money, which was going to go for those aforementioned potato chips and transistors. Remember, it wasn't as if they could just move to another part of town where rents were reasonable. So the figures couldn't be trusted and were certainly much too high. It was something like the old A-to-H quandary again, really; I mean, the Welfare certainly knew this, and so they knew the figures weren't accurate, but they still published the figures, still acted on them, and in the end probably believed them officially, since, I guess, those were the only figures they had.

It's still true, of course, that a large proportion of the families were fatherless, or there were too many fathers, or the father didn't have a vital say in the family, or wasn't the one on whom the family was dependent for a salary. What difference did it make at GW? I really couldn't see that the fact of nonexistent or nonvital dads had much to do with determining what I came to see as the definitive characteristics of The Tribe.

I'm only talking about GW, of course, which is a school for kids aged twelve to fifteen; at that age, girls everywhere are so far ahead of the boys sexually, intellectually and especially in every area that demands any kind of organization, responsibility or determination, that there is little to be seen from a comparison on the basis of father images or the lack of them.

Language, poverty, matriarchy—three platitudes about Negroes which, added together, didn't define The Tribe. Parts of each would enter into any descriptive account, of course. From language, their use of words which other American teen-agers don't commonly use in the classroom, although outside of it they use them freely enough among themselves. The Tribe swore constantly and as a matter of course. The aforementioned Sh! prefaced most remarks; hell, damn, ass (as in whip your ass), son-of-a-bitch, bitch, f———, were ordinary in all classrooms, the latter two less frequent, except when the teacher in exasperation forbade any talking at all.

Concerning poverty, certain items of property were matters of great concern, however, not because the kids didn't have them but because they did. I'll take that up in the next chapter.

The matriarchy entered in chiefly through the use of *mama* as a derisive word of the highest degree—a remark made about someone's mama made the person an object of ridicule, part of which was the result of the kid's being foolish enough to leave himself open to such a remark.

Still, they weren't an ordinary group of American teen-agers going to junior high school. Skates called them The Tribe, and the name stuck—not so much because of the verbal association with Africa, for there are plenty of other groups we commonly call tribes and not all of them are Negro, but because the group had controlling characteristics not shared by all other such groups in America, characteristics which were really at the root of their actions, and from which they could not easily escape.

(15) Apples and Oranges

I can still remember my parents telling me about Christmas
when they were children, how they used to get apples or oranges
for presents along with perhaps a toy, a doll, and maybe some
exotic nuts such as almonds or Brazil nuts which they called
niggertoes. They didn't seem to me like the kind of things you
ought to get for Christmas, and I could never work up much
feeling for them when they appeared in my stocking year after
year.

I grew up in Southern California where an orange is nothing
to get excited about—nothing suitable for a gift, hardly even
property, just an expectable part of daily life which you either
liked or didn't. My folks would relate how they would fight
about these oranges with their brothers and sisters, accusing the
others of getting more than their share. . . . How could you
fight about an old orange, I'd wonder?

During my free periods at GW these days, toward the end of
October, I began going into other classrooms to see what was
going on. We were six weeks into the season, about the time
when, in baseball, the rookies who hit 350 in spring training are
beginning to fade and be used as pinch hitters in the late innings
of ball games already won or lost. I'd begun to see that something else was needed if I was going to stay in there myself, and

I was looking for clues. However, "other classrooms" soon came to mean the shop and the art room; most classroom teachers don't like visits to their rooms, suspecting either that you are there to spy on them or to steal their secret tricks for "handling the kids." In art and shop the kids move around quite a bit, they may chatter as much as they like and approach the teacher more easily, and probably this is what makes the difference. Anyway, many of the thoughts that I'll write down in this and the next three chapters began to occur to me during this time; whatever conclusions I arrived at later on that season may as well be included here too, in a brief suspension of chronology.

Mr. Oliver, in the shop, acted like most of the shop teachers I'd known as a kid. He knew the shop was a haven for the boys and let them have their sanctuary at the cost only of observing a few rules: Do your cleanup without griping, don't misuse the tools or throw them, no honing down the files to make knives. He handed out immediate punishment with a heavy wooden paddle to offenders. He wasn't trying to change their behavior, only to control it or deal with it while they were in his shop. He also worked part time in the shop out at Juvi and was a source of information about who was there, who had been there, and even who was about to be there. Since this was a kind of official secret at GW—you never knew what had happened to a kid until he came back, unless other students told you—he was a valuable informant.

One day he told me a story about a time when a number of state or city officials were going to visit Juvi. The visit was announced in advance like Army inspections, so of course they were all getting ready to make old Juvi look pretty good. Among other things, the administration thought of lunchtime, and decided they would put bowls of fruit out on each table. Not that they didn't serve fruit regularly, of course; whatever kind was on the menu for that day, say oranges, each kid got one on his plate or at his place setting, however it was. The radical idea with the bowls consisted in the fact that the bowls would be there for the kids to help themselves from, and that there would be more than enough to go around. This last fact, Oliver said, was carefully announced in advance.

I've often wondered just what gave them this idea about the bowls of fruit. Why this particular departure from normal procedure? Perhaps they thought it looked more civilized or homelike, something like family-style in an Italian restaurant. It just seems to me an odd thing to do if you're trying especially to find things that will look good for visitors. However it was, the result was a riot.

The visiting officials were treated to the sight of the entire collection of kids rushing at the tables, grabbing fruit, sticking it inside their shirts, in their pockets, trying to run out of the dining room with it, yelling, cursing, kicking and punching each other and the counselors, breaking the bowls, mashing dropped fruit into the floor, throwing fruit in every direction when caught by group leaders . . . it took two hours to round up all the kids, lock them up, restrict them, and no one had any lunch at all. It took three more hours to clean up the dining room, and for weeks afterward rotting fruit was still being found in lockers, hidden behind furniture or in laundry bags. The visitors came to the conclusion that the kids had always been deprived of fruit at Juvi. Otherwise, they reasoned, why would anyone fight over a few oranges?

Why would a kid, or a whole row of kids, become frantic because they weren't getting any pencils? Why was it no one could pass out paper for a routine assignment without all the kids in the back rows pushing up to the front, grabbing at the paper, crumpling it and spilling it out onto the floor out of fear they wouldn't get any? Certainly it was clear by now that they were going to get paper and pencils, wasn't it? They always did, every day, every period, all year long.

It wasn't as if they even used the paper very much. In some classes very few actually wrote the assignment on that paper or even used it to doodle or write notes on or make paper planes from, and often kids left it untouched on their desks when they left; I could use it over again, or just leave it there pretending I hadn't seen it, as another little bonus for some fortunate student. Man! An extra sheet of school paper! Voices from all over the room would inform on the kid, who in turn would yell out denials and lies to protect his precious gift. If I went ahead and passed him out a sheet with all the rest, the class was shocked and outraged. He already got a piece! He got one, Mr. Herndon!

Yet plenty of kids had whole binders full of paper and those who did were quite generous with it, handing out sheets regularly to anyone who asked for it. These students with paper were indistinguishable from the rest when school paper was passed out.

Other items of property could also cause a terrible panic. Among these shoes were supreme, especially tennis shoes, which were always referred to as "tennis." Most kids carried one set of shoes around with them while wearing another pair and they were continually changing shoes in class, usually with the excuse that they were coming from or going to P.E. Tennis weren't trusted to hall or gym lockers; as in most schools, everybody knew everyone else's combinations so that the lockers were useless except as places to store absolutely worthless stuff. During class kids were continually picking up others' shoes or trying to step on new white shoes; this was especially common among girls and caused a great deal of uproar, often considerable weeping. New jackets and coats were important too and favorite shirts—let a teacher grab any kid by the collar or sleeve and he found himself facing a completely hysterical person, screaming about his clothes, his coat, his shirt, concerned only with the immediate salvation of that clothing and willing to forget any other consequence until the clothes were safe. Kids often spent entire periods simply protecting an article of clothing or a pair of tennis.

I ought to mention that we always felt it necessary to pass out one piece of paper at a time per kid. Certainly if he used it all up he might have more. But most students wanted to have two, three, several at once, in order to have a pad to write on. They didn't like to write on the bare wood of the desks and, indeed, what a pleasant, luxurious feeling it is to write on a block of paper where the pencil seems to press down on something that gives and lets the lead glide along instead of on the unyielding surface, full of cracks and carving, over which the pencil or pen makes a thin and bumpy line. But we were always aware of the remonstrances of the administration at our meetings; somehow the shortage of supplies was always crucial—running out of everything was imminent. What were we going to do in May and June, they'd be saying, if we let the kids waste materials now? Nothing is more terrifying to most teachers than the prospect of days in a classroom full of kids without supplies—no long written assignments to assure order and a period of peace and rest. We felt responsible, and on some days we could see a kid who got hold of four or five sheets of paper, wrote a little on one of them and scattered the rest on the floor as a pretty bad, heedless, irresponsible citizen, not to mention destructive and wasteful. Still, it's possible to wonder why, in all of the vast, producing, consuming, buying, advertising, fantastically wasteful country of America, it had to be precisely this one article of three-hole, blue-lined, red-margined school paper that was in short supply, which had to be carefully guarded against waste, which it was immoral to waste, which had to be parceled out one sheet at a time, equally and fairly of course, but still one at a time as if it was oranges in a region where oranges were scarce around Christmastime.

Try to narrow it down. Poverty, I've said, wasn't it. They had pocket money, most of them, and stuff bought with it. All personal property wasn't precious; their paper could be given away, money loaned, records swiped, without great outcry. Some things, though, were holy and these were mainly things that showed and looked good like the new jackets and shirts, which, once torn, were completely useless. For torn, they didn't look good, and in America you were supposed to look good, all clean, cool, sharp and above all new. There was a certain need to produce on demand, like Skates, one hundred percent of the time. Think how it would look going out there to P.E. in your brown or black street shoes, pointy-toed, high or slippery-heeled, sliding around over the floor or asphalt, the coach

asking, Where's your shoes? He (she) ain't got none! they
would all yell . . . later too, your street shoes appearing
scuffed, the shine gone, beat-up.

That was one point. But a point too was their concern over
things they didn't actually want, the paper and probably those
oranges, a concern to get their fair share of whatever was being
passed out, passed out officially, what you were spozed to get in
school, at Juvi, as an American, from the government, city,
county, from the school, from the teachers. What was being
passed out today, what probably would be passed out tomorrow, but on the other hand just might not be. What was
being passed out one at a time. For actually, of all the things
that were being passed out to them, it was always one at a time;
there never was a surplus.

There was never a surplus. In vast, producing, consuming,
wasteful America, the very image of surplus, it just happened
that all the items which were being passed out officially one by
one were those which had to be strictly guarded against misuse,
malicious destruction, and waste.

The Welfare Department, if confused about dads, certainly
knew how many people received welfare money. They knew
about the public outcry too, an outcry directed against the
parasitic and wanton folk who moved here just for those high
welfare rates. Moved right into this paradise, deliberately trying
to pay those fantastic rents, go to GW school and live two or
three families to a house with all those dads hiding out or
posing as friends of the family, just visiting.

One thing you could say for the welfare, there was never a
surplus of it. Now, you weren't going to get enough money
passed out to you, all at once, to last you for a year, or five
years, or even for six months. Can you hear them saying,
Welcome to town, and here's money in this bowl on the table
and you just get you some, enough to last awhile, pay that high
rent, buy those potato chips, get you some new tennis, and when
you get back on your feet, when your ship comes in, you can
give us back what you don't use? But you could get money
enough for one month passed out to you, according to the law,

fairly, if you could prove you didn't just come here to get that particular money, if you could prove you had to have it, if you could prove you hadn't no daddy, if you could prove you were entitled to it. Then you could get it for that month. Then, next month you could get it again, provided you could prove all those things all over again.

Forget you! one kid would often say to another if he really wished to insult him badly. It was almost as bad as calling him black. Forget you! When they said it, it was a threat and, like a magic word or a curse, a prediction—a prediction of possibilities for tomorrow, next period, next month, when it just might happen that they were going to finally forget *you*.

A definitive characteristic of The Tribe was its desire for a surplus.

(16) The Ugly Stick

As a kid of about fourteen I went to a high-school track meet with a friend of mine—I remember we went because Jesse Owens' brother was supposed to be there—and during the meet we were horsing around out on the grass when two Negro runners came loping by. One of them slapped the other or something like that, and he said, Look out, man, I'll throw some white paint on you! Both of them laughed, running past, and we thought it was one of the most hilarious things we'd ever heard. It proved to us, also, that colored guys really didn't want to be white, just as our parents were always saying, and we didn't have to do any worrying about it.

It took quite a few visits to the art room before I asked Mr. Royal about that poster welcoming everyone back to school. What I wanted to know was whether the kids at GW had made it themselves. Yeah, they did, he told me. He didn't volunteer anything else. Well, I said, it was a pretty nice poster. He nodded. Yeah, it was, wasn't it? But what I wondered, I said, was why were the two kids painted white? There hadn't seemed any other way to state the question, which was what I really wanted to know.

Mr. Royal looked at me; he didn't say much at first. Just, They all try to paint what they see. He'd been teaching there a long time, although still a young guy, a small, dark, slightly popeyed man who looked a little like Baldwin. Warming up a little, he said, I mean, like all kids, they tend to paint like pictures they've seen. I don't mean they particularly copy—some do and some don't—but they're influenced, when they paint, by the paintings or posters they've seen, not by real life. They all want to paint pictures that look like real pictures, the kind they always see.

We left it at that; Malraux had said the same thing many times in many different ways, none better, and I was surprised I hadn't thought of it.

Excluding the use of common American epithets applied to Negroes, I wrote earlier. Not that they didn't know them or use them—the point was that they applied them to themselves. Every common derisive word, all the abusive nicknames, nouns and adjectives, all the big-lip, liver-lips, burr-heads, fuzzy-heads, kinky-haired, nappy-headed, big-leg, high-ass, apes, monkeys and too-blacks were dragged out daily and heaped on each other casually or furiously, continually and fanatically. The focal point of all this was the head and color of skin, and the point was ugliness. Nose, lips, hair, all counted, but nothing else could produce the real anger of a kid being called black, or the amount of derision in the cry of watermelon-head!

The three C's alone among the kids I knew were immune from attack, being, as I say, whiter than anyone else and having fairly straight hair. The rest of the classes progressed through the traditional black, brown and beige, and the blacker a kid was, the kinkier his hair, the wider and flatter his nose, the larger and more everted his lips, the uglier he was and the more crap he had to take. Robert he got hit with the ugly stick, Mr. Hern-don, some kid would yell, and that was that for Robert. When it dark outside nobody can't even see Fletcher! Watch out somebody don't steal your head for a watermelon!

My own classes ran true to form. 7B rarely indulged in this sort of insult, 8B constantly, but surreptitiously, because they thought I'd disapprove and it would show up in their grades, 9D constantly and openly because their free gift was such that they did what they wanted to, and 7H whenever they could get their minds off their own problems long enough to remember to attack someone else. At first I was extremely surprised and shocked. I couldn't imagine how, with a whole white world ready and willing to call them all these names and always making the distinction between African-looking (ugly) Negroes and Caucasian-looking (handsome) Negroes, they could add to the situation themselves.

For a time I began to think that it was all a subtle way of finding out about me—if they said, for instance, that somebody was big-lipped, fuzzy-headed, black and therefore ugly, was I going to somehow agree that he was uglier than the rest? Then I could be exposed as a racist, just another white mother, and could be dismissed. But as it kept on, day after day, all year long, even after they had in many cases ceased to pay any attention to me at all for long periods of time, I could see it wasn't for my benefit. It was for themselves.

It never stopped. It was a characteristic of The Tribe. They agreed that qualities which they all shared to some degree from birth were to add up to *bad*. It was crucial that they join the people most hostile to them all in order to establish relative degrees of ugliness, in order that some might be less ugly. I got over my surprise, got over trying to figure if it was meant for me, and it soon became only very boring, like slightly risqué jokes schoolkids are always telling you which you've heard a hundred times. You couldn't ever say anything about dark, black, brown, gray, shadow, night, head, nose, mouth, feet, legs, no raccoons, no dancing of jigs, no spades, no skin, without invoking hoots of laughter and a number of personal remarks. No one could read about any melons (your head look like one), no one could read about apes or monkeys (you look like one) . . . and if you somehow managed to avoid all that, the rhymes would get you. Say crack, back, track, Mac, hack, and you'd soon hear, Teacher, did you say black? or May, Mr. Herndon say you too black! Or there would be the bitter variation, Robert, go on leave me alone! You too white (quite, flight, bright, knight and right). Whooo-eee!

Times had changed, it seemed, since the track meet. White paint was now in favor. If I had imagined that the students of GW would present a united front on the question of their own (relative) blackness, it was a mistake. If I had supposed they were concerned with testing me, that was a mistake too. They weren't interested in degrees of liberal white attitudes like they spozed to be. No, just let the cry of *watermelon-head!* ring out through the classrooms of The Tribe and you knew that somebody was making a poster, painting himself white if only for a moment, even if only relatively . . . painting himself into the good, white side like any other artist.

(17) The Plop Reflex

It was Opal Jameson who introduced me to the third major characteristic of The Tribe. Opal was a member of 7B and ordinarily no member of that class would have been caught dead indulging himself, at least in the classroom, in any of the characteristics of The Tribe. Except for Opal. Opal was a big, tall, very black, strong girl with bad-luck features; she was aggressive, argumentative, headstrong, unable to endure criticism of the mildest sort, uncooperative and, at the same time, very intelligent indeed—which was why she was still hanging on in the B group. I didn't think she'd remain there throughout the next two years at GW, but as it turned out of course, I never found out.

Opal's desire was to be my second-in-command. If allowed to pass out the paper, collect the work, correct the spelling papers, call out the assignment, check the book numbers and do all the various small administrative jobs in the classroom, she was happy, did her own work and didn't cause no trouble. Unfortunately she didn't always get to do this. First of all, these were big status jobs and many other kids in class wanted to share the glory; and second, she became so officious and overbearing in her performance of these duties—she argued with the kids about the neatness or the heading or the correctness of the work they were turning in, she moralized constantly about the scarcity of school materials and the evils of waste, she marked spelling words wrong if kids forgot to dot their i's—that we couldn't bear it all the time. When refused her prerogatives, she would consistently embark on some sort of antisocial behavior upon which I would have to comment; at the comment she would begin to argue, getting louder and louder and angrier and angrier until I would have to tell her to shut up and sit down. She would refuse to do this in no uncertain terms, whereupon I'd have to make a threat or advance toward her, at which point she would resort to the Plop Reflex.

My introduction to the reflex came about the third week of school, about two weeks before the time now, that I'm writing about, when I was thinking about The Tribe. It was apparently the time in which kids' hopes had about run out for another year, leaving about forty more weeks to go. Up until this time Opal had been happily doing all these administrative tasks for me, and I was quite happy to have someone do them, but it was brought to my attention by other kids that lots of students wanted to do these jobs, that why should Opal always get to do them, especially since Opal didn't always behave very well in class, and that it wasn't fair. We discussed this in class and I can now imagine Opal listening to this with no very good feeling—no doubt it happened just like this every year. In the end, a little boy named Lorenzo was chosen to pass out paper the next day, and people got started making schedules and monitor lists and all that.

The next day I started talking about the Indians and the Bering Strait and something about Kon-Tiki, I remember, for we were reading about the Indians who used to live nearby, the oak trees which were all over, the shell mounds the Indians left by the bay, and by and by I announced an assignment in the book. Opal got up to pass out the paper. Immediately Lorenzo let out a yell that he was supposed to do it. I agreed that he was right. Opal simply said Sh!, grabbed the paper, and started up the row with it. I told her to stop and give it to Lorenzo, about half Opal's size, who was standing up by his seat, waiting for justice. Opal ignored me and started thumbing off sheets of paper and slapping them on desks. I insisted. She slammed all the paper down on the floor and advanced upon me. She had a peculiar stance when arguing: her feet flat on the floor, chin thrust out, her body following it, leaning over, her butt stuck way out in back of her, arms hanging straight down at her sides, so that she looked like a V standing on one of its legs. Well, Lorenzo already asked, I said, and it was already decided yesterday. She knew it. She said that Lorenzo didn't know how to do it, all the paper would be wasted, that she was spozed to do it, that I was just mad at her and wouldn't let her do it. Finally, argument not availing, she marched over to the kid, who, during the arguing, had been picking up all the paper and was just beginning to pass it out, and tried to snatch it away from him. The class began to protest. Anarchy threatened. I wasn't about to have my only reasonable class going crazy. Shut up and sit down, Opal! I yelled. You are not passing out the paper. That's that! Opal, all hope lost, let out a yell, launched herself backward exactly as if she were a diver beginning a back one-and-a-half, flew into the air, bounced off a desk and came down right square on her head on the floor and lay there.

And that was the Plop Reflex. Remember how in the old comic strip, *Mutt and Jeff,* some situation would be set up, something would happen and then, by a twist, turn out unexpectedly? The one, usually Mutt, the smart one, would be so amazed, so astounded, so flabbergasted by the utter illogic of events, the insanity of the situation and the stupidity of Jeff that he would simply keel over with astonishment; the implication was that everything was so absurd that no other action was left open to him. It always happened in the last frame of the cartoon and all you saw were the feet and part of the legs of Mutt, off the ground, disappearing out of the frame, and in the air above the feet and legs was always written the word PLOP!

Of course it wasn't Opal who really introduced the Plop Reflex to me but Ruth that first day. But at the time I hadn't thought of it as a characteristic of The Tribe, but only as a little added attraction of Ruth's. As a characteristic, in action, it was limited to the girls; not only that, but to the blacker, more African-looking girls—those of the ugly stick. It just wouldn't have done for a brown-skinned, straight-haired, thin-nosed chick to be hurtling through the air like that. Just the same, it was definitive; everyone shared in it, although only certain individuals were chosen to perform it.

Its significance? I'd say it was terror. When all hope was lost, when no one was going to understand, when your demand wasn't going to be satisfied (even if that demand was impossible of satisfaction)—then you could resort to terror. At least that's what I felt and what The Tribe felt when the girls landed on their heads with a bang. Possibilities, justice—none of it counted just then, and your momentary terror came as a reflex too, a reaction to an event which had just rendered you powerless.

(18) Colleagues

Teachers are always willing to give advice to new (or old) teachers, and I talked to them all during those first six or seven weeks. The advice was of two kinds. The first kind was useful enough and was about methods and equipment you could use to do certain things—sets of flash cards, how to group students, controlled readers, recorders, easily corrected tests, good films —but after a short time I was already using most of these. My problem was not what to use but how to get the kids to respond in such a way that they learned something. That brought up the other kind of advice, which was also the most common and which was useless to me. This advice was a conglomeration of dodges, tricks, gimmicks to get the kids to do what they were spozed to do, that is, whatever the teacher had in mind for them to do. It really involved a kind of gerrymandering of the group— promises, favors, warnings, threats, letting you pass out or not pass out paper, sit in a certain place or not, A's, plusses, stars, and also various methods for getting the class working before they knew it. The purpose of all these methods was to get and keep an aspect of order, which was reasonable enough, I suppose. But the purpose of this order was supposed to be so that "learning could take place." So everyone said—not wanting to be guilty of the authoritarian predilection for order for its own sake—while at the same time admitting that most of the kids weren't learning anything this way. Everyone agreed that our students were on the average a couple of years below grade level, everyone agreed that was because they were "deprived" kids, but no one agreed that simply because nothing was going on the way they were doing it, they ought to try something else.

It's not my purpose or even desire to criticize these teachers —they were as good or better than most and they had a difficult job—but frankly I could never come to terms with their attitude. They knew a certain way, or ways, to teach. They knew how to get control of the class and, that established, some ways to present the material they thought important. The control didn't work consistently because the kids were not easily threatened, having little to lose. Promises were fairly successful at the beginning of the year, but their power steadily declined as the kids saw through them or were disillusioned about their value. The material which was so important, which had to be "covered," was supposed to lead toward understanding, broader knowledge, scientific method, good citizenship or, more specifically, toward better writing, speech, figuring, grammar, geography, whatever it was. But actually what was happening was that they were presenting the students, every day, with something for them either to do or not-do, while keeping them through order from any other alternative. If a kid couldn't or wouldn't do his assignment, he had only the choice of not-doing it, of doing nothing. Almost every teacher admitted that this last was the choice of half the class on any given day.

The kids who chose to do the assignment seemed rarely to benefit from it; even if they did the speller conscientiously, their written work remained badly spelled. The A's promised as prize for hard work didn't materialize. The result was that these teachers faced, every year, the certain knowledge that the first day of school was the best they could hope for, since the progress and morale of the class could only be downhill. The only question left was whether or not they could hold out.

Following this point in our talks, such as they were, would

flow generalities of analysis and interpretation. Since their teaching methods were right in other schools, they argued, it must be the fact of "deprivation" which was at fault here. Deprivation was identified as a problem now, and problems were supposed to be dealt with in such a way that they ceased to exist. If deprivation was hindering learning, then someone should do something about that deprivation.

What to do? The first and best thing, they all knew, was education. With education would come better skills, with skills would come better jobs, with better jobs would come middle-class incomes and the attendant middle-class mores, values and ideas of order. After that the school program, curriculum and methods, being essentially right, would work since the reason they didn't work now was that the students were of the wrong kind; *i.e.,* they were deprived.

But how were they to get educated, The Tribe, if the education they were getting right here and now wasn't working? How get these skills (values, ideas of order) if the methods used to teach them weren't producing any skills by and large? I hate to keep saying this, but the inescapable fact is that they weren't working and that therefore the rest was simply nonsense.

Long before we met, my wife had worked for Dr. Thomas French at the Institute for Psychoanalysis in Chicago, and during this time I was reading the first volume of his book *The Integration of Behavior,* which he had sent her. He planned, in a series of books, to generalize about human behavior, in terms of its being integrated or "goal-directed," from a case history of an "abnormal" personality; in one place he answered critics, who complained that you can't attribute the mechanisms of abnormality to the normal ways of behavior, by stating and giving numerous examples of the fact that the component re-actions "such as are necessary to account for" normal behavior play an essential part in neurotic or abnormal (or deprived) behavior. The disintegration of reactions in abnormal behavior seemed to show up goals and processes in a kind of relief, and motivational patterns which might be overlooked in normal behavior were clearly shown in the abnormal. In terms of my talks with colleagues, I began to use this idea to include what they thought of as the normal (middle-class) and the abnormal (The Tribe's) reactions to their methods of teaching, and to think that The Tribe's reaction to this teaching was not different, only more overt, violent, and easily seen than that of this imaginary normal or "non-deprived" child. In short that where the middle-class kids were learning enough outside of the classroom or accepting the patterns of conformity and behavior more readily and easily so as to make it seem that they were actually learning in school, The Tribe, unable to do this, was exposing the system as ineffective for everyone. It wasn't working for them, it wasn't working for anyone, I felt; only with The Tribe, it was more painful when it didn't work.

This kind of thing is what I hoped to avoid in these pages, but really I don't see that it can be avoided entirely. After awhile I just talked with the teachers about baseball, places to eat dinner, good movies, the pleasantries of everyday life, so that where I had been well on my way to being a difficult person to talk to, objecting to everything, I came to be a friendly and talkative man (I think) who, to be sure, was having his troubles in his first year of teaching at GW.

Skates indulged himself as usual in the teachers' room. His main interest was in the Negro teachers, and he was always disappointed in them for failing to be revolutionary in nature. He expected them to be in constant conflict with their society and especially to keep on talking about it. He was the only teacher at GW who ever alluded to the fact that some people in the world and even some teachers and students at GW were members of the Negro race and that this race had its difficulties in contemporary America. If a Negro teacher mentioned that he'd flown somewhere, Skates would immediately inquire which airline and go into a polemic about certain airlines which didn't fly Negroes. It always infuriated him when no one else would admit any knowledge of such a situation.

The Negro teachers were always going out, on weekends, to a

country club to swim or play golf or, as Skates always put it, just to be in a country club. Whenever they talked about it on Mondays—only wanting to mention what a good time they'd had, how many martinis they'd drunk or what their golf scores had been—Skates would demand to know where this club was. It turned out that it was way out of town somewhere, a long distance anyway, and then Skates would demand to know why they went all the way out there when there were plenty of good country clubs closer to home. Since the reason was that the club was the only one around that would admit Negroes, his questioning made everyone extremely nervous. Occasionally Skates would change tactics and say he'd like to go out to the club with them sometime, if, he wondered aloud, they were sure the club would admit Jews. So many of them, he'd say, didn't.

He never stopped pushing them like this; still, he was also a very cheerful and humorous guy at times as well as being extremely flirtatious with the women, so that the teachers both feared and desired his presence at their tables for lunch.

The only other teacher I knew well was Mr. Brooks; we were associated mainly because he, like myself, didn't really know what he was doing and because we both had 7H to cope with. Brooks had planned to be a coach, but right now he was teaching arithmetic while waiting for an opening in the P.E. department with the district. He was quite a pleasant guy and quite often he and Skates and I played basketball together out on the field after school with whatever kids were still hanging around, and after the game we would tell each other horrible stories about 7H.

Brooks had the right idea for GW though. He planned to control 7H, keep them quiet and in their seats. He had one thing going for him in this respect; he'd played football in college and had had offers to join a professional training camp which he'd turned down in order to start teaching. Thus he was a big, rough guy and he had a notebook of his press clippings which he kept on his desk for the boys to read and this helped. It didn't help enough though, and for quite a while he used to show up at my classroom door just before the end of school in order to keep 7H after school a little. I could always tell when he was coming, because the kids always knew. After spending a great deal of time loudly pinning the blame on one kid or another—the kid denying it, of course, and pointing to other culprits—they would start in making statements about what they would do when Brooks arrived, how nobody keep them after school, etc. Brooks would arrive just before the bell looking solemn or angry. The bell would ring. You ain't keeping me! someone, usually Roy or Alexandra, would shout. I am, Brooks would say. No you ain't, I'm leaving now! the kid would yell. Try it, Brooks would say, and then Roy, say, would run full speed across the room and hurl himself at Brooks, who would hurl him back effortlessly, and then someone else would rush him. It became a game, a ritual; the kids never got tired of it, since they weren't going anywhere anyway. Brooks, however, did tire of it after a while and figured out something else, or didn't. This was during October, as I've said; after that I lost track of what he was doing, as I lost track of almost everything about GW except what went on in my own room with my own students. But the one thing in Brooks's favor at GW was that he was determined to keep order; Grissum could see that he was trying and that eventually he'd learn how to do it. Since he also made himself available for all kinds of extra yard and playground duty—to Skates's disgust—he was judged an up-and-coming man.

Old Mrs. Z down the hall, next door to Skates, was the real wonder of the school. I'm not pretending she was typical. For a while I was interested in where 9D went after they left my room, and as this happened to be to Mrs. Z for arithmetic, I used to go down and talk to her. She was white-haired, apparently frail, and Southern. She told me that she had a very simple attitude toward her students which was in fact no different from her feelings about people in general. That was, all her life she'd spoken only to people who were ladies and gentlemen. Since none of the students of 9D were ladies and gentlemen, she never spoke to them, never had, and never would. She also forbade them to speak in her classroom, for the same reason. If they did speak she sent them immediately to the office with a note instructing the office to keep them for the period. If they left their seats, she did the same. If they chewed gum, put on lipstick or changed their shoes, out they went. She didn't even speak to them when they were kicked out—just handed them the slip from a ready stack inside her desk which she had all filled out except the name of the culprit and the infraction of which he was guilty. Those left in the room on any given day did in fact sit still and quiet; otherwise, of course, they just weren't there. Mrs. Z felt that, not being ladies and gentlemen who could be trusted to behave themselves in any situation without regulation, they must obey orders and if they didn't even do that, they should not be in her room.

Above her desk on the wall she had erected, many years ago, a shelf on which she placed her files of ditto masters containing the problems on adding, subtracting, percentage, decimals, ratios, square roots, areas, perimeters, formulas, the whole kit and kaboodle of ninth-grade arithmetic. These she ran off, one a day, handed out the copies one at a time to 9D and her other classes for them to do or not-do, and collected them at the end of the period, done or not-done. All explanation was contained in the ditto. She herself spent the period between sending out disobedient students, correcting the previous day's work and noting the non-work, and that ditto was handed back with corrections, a percentage, and a grade. The grade she entered in her own book.

In a way, Mrs. Z was magnificent. If she was not typical of the rest of the teachers at GW, it was mainly because she was capable of a far-reaching logic and basically confident. I felt that the attitudes of the rest were not basically different, only that their methods were incomplete. They too wanted the kids absolutely quiet and orderly, only instead of just eliminating them from the class they argued and moralized with them about it, an activity which resulted in no order and also no change in student attitude or behavior. They also wanted the kids to do classroom assignments regularly and to do only that work chosen by them, the teachers, the difference again being only that they tried to talk the kids into doing the work, or to encourage them, or promise them something for it. That is only an admission to the children that there could be some disagreement about whether the rule or the assignment is proper, old Mrs. Z said to me often out there in the hall, and that is of course not true. There is absolutely no point, she continued, in encouraging the children to believe something that is not true. At least, that's the way she saw it.

Another person I often talked with was the school secretary, especially around this time when I started receiving some notes from downtown about which I'll write later. She had been there a long time, knew all about past administrations and all the current gossip about the kids and teachers. One day she gave me a ride downtown to the district office; perhaps I'd ridden to work with Skates, forgetting I had to go down there, or maybe my car wasn't running. Anyway, as we passed the lake talking about this and that, she suddenly said quite savagely, There's the bastard now!

I was a little surprised at that, but also I couldn't see who the bastard was. Where? I asked. There, she said, slowing down and pointing to a big, new building going up in front of us.

I thought it was the new Kaiser building, and said so. That's right! she cried, Henry J. Kaiser, the man who caused all our troubles. He's the one brought in all these niggers in the first place!

(19) Brotherhood Week

It was announced in our teachers' meeting that the last week in October was going to be designated Brotherhood Week throughout the district. The UN, One World, new nations arising to take their places, etc., equality, were to be emphasized. Certain special films were scheduled to be shown in connection with this in the English and Social Studies classes.

I showed them all. One was a film starring Frank Sinatra. Frank was making a record as the film opened, and he just happened to step outside the studio for a little breather when a gang of bad kids rushed up, chasing a scrawny, scared, little Polish kid. The Polish kid was pretty foreign-looking—odd clothes, dark hair and skin, big nose. Old Frank talked to the bad kids about things like the melting pot and how they all came from somewhere else (although presumably not from Poland), and at the end of the film the kids all felt pretty liberal and the Polish kid was accepted into the gang and they went off to play ball and Frank went back into the studio. There he sang a song that had been quite popular back in the early forties when The Tribe hadn't been born. It's barely possible that this kind of lecture by Bobby Blue Bland might have impressed the kids, but Sinatra didn't make it for them.

Another of our films was an avant-garde cartoon called

Boundary Lines. I liked it. When I said so, the kids told me I was crazy, because that film was crazy.

In contrast, the third film caused quite a stir. It was about the UN on a kind of youth level. Kids of all nations, that was the idea, and it opened up with a title shot of kids' heads framed around a circle. There were various Caucasians in national headgear so you could tell them apart; there was an Oriental, an Indian, what looked like an Eskimo, and, right in the middle, one big, shiny, black face.

Brothers, said the film out loud. The classes broke up. Who that one? they all wanted to know. No brother to me! Teacher, that Robert's brother, he an ape too! Everybody laughed like hell. You mean they spozed to like that kid too? No, man! Of all the ugly kids they'd ever seen, he was the ugliest. Get him out of here! Whooo-eee!

If that was the way the UN was going to act, trying to include them apes, they didn't think much of its chances in the modern world.

(20) *Laid Off*

My heroic and illegal efforts at State and Berkeley that last summer had paid off by my meeting the credential requirements on the nose, but all of a sudden I realized that there was a deadline for sending the papers in to the state and I hadn't met it. I hurried around collecting documents and signatures and, just in time, I thought, fired them off to the district office downtown, which in turn was to do something to them and send them on to the state.

The next I heard from them was in a letter from the Board of Education in Los Angeles, informing me that the papers had arrived there by mistake and that its office had kindly sent them back to San Diego! I wrote some frantic letters and made some calls to the district office, which seemed to think I had deliberately confused the matter and was making a lot of trouble for everyone. Several days later during my free period I was summoned to Mr. Grisson's office, where he regretfully informed me that my papers hadn't arrived in Sacramento in time and that therefore I was actually uncertified to teach at GW or anywhere else at the moment, and would have to stop doing it until everything was cleared up. A young lady who had been substituting in the district had been called in to take my classes for the month of November; after that, it was hoped I could resume my work.

That was that. I made a trip that weekend to Sacramento and rambled around the big, new, glass-walled Education Building until I found a lady who, for a fact, had my papers and letters right in front of her. She was friendly and deplored the whole thing. In vain I urged her to certify the papers then and there, but nothing doing. Something about time limitations and regulations—the letter laying me off had been written before the papers arrived, or at least, probably; it was another department that wrote the letters, and once laid off, you had to remain laid off for at least a month. After all, she said, you did delay sending in the documents until the last moment. I couldn't deny it. It was a simple penalty, not much different from the one you faced if you forgot to hide Dad under the bed one month when the Welfare people came around. I made the rounds of a few Sacramento bars to console myself and drove home.

Still, it wasn't too bad, I reasoned. My wife and I were both angry and disgusted—she with me, and I with myself. However, I still had the job. My papers were OK, the lady said, just late, and I could go back to work in December after missing out on a month's pay. For luck, I'd already applied for Christmas work at the post office and I very soon got a call to start working four hours a day, so we almost made it financially.

Congratulations, man! Skates told me. You got out of GW for a while! Well, that was true. I rested up, cased mail at the P.O. in the evenings, and began to try to think what I was going to do when I got back, for actually in the last month and a half with 7H and 9D I had come almost to the end of my rope.

＊

(21) What To Do?

Casing mail at the post office, you've plenty of time to think, in contrast to teaching school at GW where there's no time to think at all. Sometime during that month of comparative leisure I began to ask myself what I had taught to the students of 7H and 9D; the answer was that as far as I could see I'd taught them nothing.

I also thought about 7B and 8B, and dismissed them again for the same reason as before—they weren't crucial. I thought I was doing all right with 7B. They were doing the work, of course, I was following along the course outline, for after all they had to join an eighth-grade class next year which would expect them to know things like what is an adverb and who discovered Monterey Bay, and we had intelligent and hard-hitting discussions about the effects of some of this history on various groups who lived in America like the Indians or Chinese, we did a lot of writing and editing and reading aloud of their own work according to my composition plan—all in all we were having a pleasant and useful time in the classroom, I thought. I decided I wasn't exactly selling them out.

8B would get along without me well enough. They were committed to a simple ideal, which was to pretend interest in and conformity to the status quo, in order to secretly sabotage it. They hoped to advance in the world while still indulging themselves in its destruction. In a sense, I couldn't argue; they were attempting to con their way through, disbelieving in any other possibility, and perhaps it was as practical a way as any I might have to offer.

7B believed in what they'd been told ever since kindergarten—the school ideals, neatness, promptness, courtesy, hard work; perform according to them, they'd been told, and you could grow up to be President or at least a private secretary (private secretaries were, according to the girls, the most enviable girls alive) and enjoy the promise of middle-class America. Believing this and being on the whole quite intelligent, they were a cheerful bunch in class, which was where they saw their hope, order, and future. I hoped they were right.

In any case, to get either group around to another way of thinking—and remember that 7B wasn't more *correct* in their analysis of the world than 8B, just a hell of a lot pleasanter to be with—would require a tremendous amount of time and energy, which, given the existence of 7H and 9D, I just didn't have; also, just what was the correct view of the world, of history, of the California Indians, of Basic English, of GW for that matter? Both 7B and 8B were coping with their grades, for proof of which they were still in B groups, and that's all they needed to do and all I could expect them to do. Both had divined the absolute key to getting through school, namely, that you must understand and somehow satisfy the bureaucracy. One group understood it and trusted it; the other understood it and conned it. Either way the bureaucracy was satisfied. It didn't distinguish between 7B and 8B because they were both B.

So my commitment was irrevocably to 7H and 9D, who weren't coping. The commitment, apparently, wasn't enough; nothing was going on. We'd established the preliminaries, or what I thought of as the preliminaries—who we were in there, how we were going to act—and we should have been ready to go. Why weren't we?

Well, I told myself, for one thing, 7H was in no shape to learn or do anything. The heart of their problem as a class was the simple skill of reading. There were four kids who couldn't read their own names, three or four who couldn't read anything else, and the rest of the class who could read a little but were always shaky about it. They were unsure if they would be able to avoid derision at any given moment, and so tried to assert their superiority over each other in the very area of their common incompetence. Any time we tried to work on beginning word recognition, letters, sounds, the majority sounded off about "that baby stuff," and as a result the nonreaders had to sound off about it too; they couldn't admit not knowing how to read and so they couldn't ever begin to learn, because in order to learn they'd have to begin, right there in class, with simplicities, easily identified by all as "learning to read," and open themselves up to scorn. Nothing doing.

On the other hand, everything we were supposed to be doing in class presupposed that everybody could read. The Word (now in a third sense, as *Logos*)—that was all that was going on in school, the beginning and the end, only here it was the printed word. If you couldn't read it, what could you do?

7H had quite a few answers to that. Confronted with the word, Roy, for instance, laughed. He jumped up, threw back his head and laughed. He advanced to my desk and laughed, he roared with laughter, he raced around the room laughing. Everything was so funny he couldn't stop laughing long enough to read. Vincent got nervous. His face broke out in red blotches, and his eyes watered so badly that he had to take out his handkerchief and wipe them, so that of course the only reason he couldn't read was that his eyes were watering so—otherwise, he implied, he could read the hell out of it. Harvey always looked at me indignantly and asked why did I always pick on him to read the hardest parts? Now them other easy parts, I could read them real good, he'd say, but you just trying to make me read all the hard parts and I ain't going to do it!

Alexandra alone faced the reading issue with defiance and aplomb—she read like hell. Whatever was given to her, she just read right along, stumbling occasionally, but always recovering and getting everything right. This drove me crazy until I discovered that she was listening to Judy sitting right behind her muttering the words and Alexandra, sharp and cool, reading aloud after her. So I moved Judy one day, and Alexandra still read right along although considerably slower and with some mistakes; she not only had to be looking over at Judy in order to read her lips, but she also had to look down at the page once in awhile to give a semblance of reality and it was pretty difficult. She read Judy's lips! It's not so astounding, I guess; they'd been together in classes for years so Alexandra had had lots of practice. On days when Judy was absent Alexandra just pulled potato chips or candy out of her purse before her turn and began to eat them ostentatiously. If this didn't prompt a remark from me the other kids would object loudly; Alexandra would then begin to argue about eating in class (her mama *told* her to eat them potato chips!) and pretty soon Alexandra would get mad and announce how she wasn't going to do no reading today because I was so mean!

On the first day I found out she was reading Judy's lips, I went slightly crazy; I lectured her for ten minutes on how difficult it was to read lips, how simple it was by comparison to read, how if she'd have spent one-tenth of the time learning to read that she'd spent avoiding it . . . finally she yelled out furiously that she could so read, and why was I trying to lie and say she couldn't read? Judy piped up and said she was Alexandra's best friend and she ought to know, and Alexandra could so read, and that she—Judy—just read along with Alexandra to keep her company because we friends, Mr. Herndon! The rest of the class was taking sides by that time and began advising me on what Alexandra had done in the second or fifth grades and what *that* teacher said and did; finally someone remembered that I'd mentioned the secret word *lips* and said no wonder Alexandra could read Judy's lips, they were so big and fat and ugly, and so we had to hear from all sides about big-lip and liver-lip and watermelon-head and so on down the line. During this time Alexandra gained the upper hand, having very thin lips, and Judy, for all her fat-lip, could read better than anyone else. So everything was fine, except we were right back where we began.

The other nonreaders, or almost nonreaders, applied similar tactics, to the effect that it was more honorable to appear bad than stupid. When it came their turns to read they simply did something outrageous, we had our uproar, got over it, and Virgil or Judy would finish reading the story.

At one point I decided to get Judy and Virgil to help teach the others. It was the obvious thing to do and was fine in one sense—that is, everyone knew that Virgil and Judy were smart, smarter than anyone else in the class by a long shot, and so it was no disgrace to be instructed by them. Everyone was happy to cooperate. I had Virgil and Judy sitting at desks turned around to face three or four other desks, all equipped with flash cards, simple sentences written on large sheets, syllable sounds, rhyming words—everything all set, just as the unit plans say. I stood by, ready to lend a hand and also to keep the rest of the class busy or at least fairly quiet. Everyone enjoyed it a lot, but it didn't work.

The trouble was Virgil and Judy. Judy was a short, stocky little girl, black, African-looking, intelligent, and she possessed a terrible impatience and a temper. For one thing, having had to take everybody's crap for so long about her looks, she was not going to hold back pointing out their lacks in the area of brains. She liked being teacher, and often worked at it quite seriously, but she almost always went too fast, got impatient, criticized, mocked and called everyone stupid, which no one could take without making a remark in turn about Judy's head.

Virgil hadn't changed any since the first day, which makes it obvious how his group went. He showed them a word and then told them it meant something else; he wrote long words or nonsense words and slipped them into the stack of flash cards, or else he would ask Wade or Harvey how to spell antidisestab-lishmentarianism—and of course the ability to spell that word, in no matter what school, always represents the acme of intelligence and culture.

While this was going on, he advised them not to consult me because I was still trying to figure out ways to get them in trouble; this kept them where he wanted them, in a place where there was no appeal, no chance to find out anything for certain. He didn't even want them to trust *him*—Virgil wanted above all a permanent state of uneasiness for everyone. He was simply a mean little son-of-a-bitch, no matter how he got that way. We still had, by the way, the problem with the absence slips. Most days now I let Alexandra copy the names on the slips themselves, using the printed class list on my desk. I would check the ones for her to copy and she wrote them down and posted the slips. They could tell their names if Alexandra wrote them down, apparently, and of course trusted her since she was in the same boat. It was a long process though, and once in awhile something in the class would prevent me from enlisting Alexandra's help and I'd have to turn the slips in myself. Whenever I refused Alexandra, they were all certain that I was plotting against them, even though in fact they never got into trouble about it.

Skates said that the trouble with the class—I kept describing it to him and worrying about it—was that it was like a concentration camp. You got all kinds thrown in there together, he said, for all different reasons. You got honest-to-God crooks, you got politicals, and some just plain old Jews. You can't figure out what the camp is really for! What was the H for? I assumed it was a classification for the ten or twelve in the class who were reading and writing at about a second- or third-grade level, just keeping out of the basement. But if so, that left out Roy, *et al.*, who weren't necessarily slow learners or necessarily anything else—you simply couldn't tell, at least not by the goddam tests since they couldn't read them. So the inclusion of Roy, Vincent, Harvey and Alexandra and the four others who were almost as bad made it a class for nonreaders, a place to take up reading from the beginning, *i.e.*, the alphabet.

Still, with Virgil and Judy that H changed again; it designated a category for smart kids who had temper tantrums or were sons-of-bitches, a kind of opportunity class, as we called it when I was in grammar school, where intolerable kids could either straighten up or rot while keeping out of everyone's hair.

What to do? One thing was to send Judy and Virgil to the library to work by themselves, but they weren't easily shut out of things, and after one visit to the library the librarian wouldn't have them in again. Also, the nonreaders refused to work with anyone but Judy or Virgil. They weren't going to be instructed by some kid who could just barely read himself, since that made their position too obvious. Again, I couldn't work at all with just the slow readers, the majority of the class, for that meant that I was implying that those left out couldn't read, which was of course intolerable. There we were, crooks, politicals and Jews, stuck with each other, and I couldn't for the life of me figure out any plan that was going to take care of them all.

How did the kids feel about it? Guessing, I'd say that the slow readers, the majority, were the least satisfied. At least their complaints were the most reasonable and the most consistent. We ain't learning anything, Mr. Herndon! Why don't you teach us nothing? You spozed to teach us that book!—pointing to *Red Feather* or some other damfool piece of printed matter. I couldn't tell if they really meant it, but I agreed with the complaint. Virgil and Judy were happy. They allowed themselves all kinds of liberties of temper and deceit, were looked upon as geniuses, and received attention from all sides. The nonreaders, while I suppose generally miserable all the time, appeared to like the class; perhaps it tormented them less than other situations they'd been in.

All in all, they were probably enjoying themselves. There was lots of activity, lots of excitement and uproar for which no one was being sent to Miss Bentley, and there was lots going on that looked like really seventh-grade school. The grouping-instruction arrangements were a tremendous success, what with the moving of desks, the cards, slips of paper, colors, the grand passing out of all these materials . . . it wasn't at all boring for them. As Harvey remarked right in the middle of things one day, This look like a real class! It is a real class, you watermelon-head! came the retort from someone. I know it a real class, said Harvey stubbornly, but I mean it look like it is too!

Well, it did look like one (at least to me and Harvey) but still we weren't getting anywhere. At least, that's how I saw it there in the post office. What to do?

9D wasn't the same. They didn't have the problems of the nonreading population of 7H, nor, of course, did they have Judy and Virgil. It wasn't entirely clear why they were in the D section—but the middle section in any such system is the most unclear as to reasons why. They hadn't serious enough problems to keep them from being able to read, say, but then neither were they with it enough to keep doing homework and write compositions and join the B's. They were in many ways the most mature of the school population, but also the most apathetic and disinterested and cynical about the entire range of school activities. What had we done in 9D?

As I said, we'd been intellectuals. That means we discussed all serious questions with a view to finding out the reasons and causes and probable outcomes of situations, everyone having a say including myself. The discussions were lively, honest, uncompromising (and disorderly)—I was on the whole satisfied with them. The problem with such discussions was they inevitably came to an end. Like intellectuals everywhere, we demanded action, but—again, like many—we found none to take and became inevitably disgusted with all this talk. A good example of this was our discussion about the meaning of D and of the whole grouping arrangement.

Although the kids were supposed to be unaware of the existence and nature of the grouping arrangement, they of course knew all about it. One day a kid opened up a period by asking me to explain why they were all in a dumb class—what he actually said, I remember, was If we in this dumb class why should we do anything if we already too dumb to do it? Yeah, came a number of voices in agreement, old D for Dumb! and several similar expressions. This particular discussion went on for several days and I recall being pleased that there was this carry-over from one period to the next, and the students came in the next day ready to take up where they'd finished the day before. It was also one of the few times they wanted to listen to me talk for long periods of time, which was perhaps why I remember it so well. I tried to explain about the tests, who made them, who took them, what they meant or didn't mean, why you might do well or badly on them on any given day, and how they got the groups out of the results of the tests. We figured out the ratios on the board—everyone could do this exercise although they all flunked arithmetic—in short we covered the subject completely. Everyone wanted to know about it because, I imagine, it was true and had something to do with them, and no one had ever gone into it with them before. However, at the end of it there remained the same old problem, what to do? All the talk hadn't changed anything; they were still in old D for Dumb and they were going to stay there. As soon as someone came up with this pronouncement the discussion stopped, the end being forcibly expressed as usual by Verna's turning her back on me and the class and saying Sh! May *et al.*, clamored once again for spellers so's they could learn what they spozed to, but they were yelled down by others who shouted that they'd been doing those old spellers and those sentences for years and hadn't gotten out of the dumb class yet—they could see that wasn't the way. That was about the way things stood. We'd talked about everything, about what was wrong with everything, but when we finished, all those things were still wrong. We had to do something, but what that was we didn't know. As a class we only knew what we didn't want to do, what we weren't going to do because it wasn't no use to do it.

At the post office I could think about all this very clearly in quite abstract terms and I narrowed the problem down to its primary causes. Why was 7H different from 7B? Not that they weren't as smart or hadn't learned certain useful skills about school; that was true enough but wasn't the problem. The problem wasn't how to get them to be as smart as 7B but simply to get them to begin learning as much as they could right now, however much that might be. The difference was one of solidarity as a class. 7B had it, they felt good as a class, and so each one could go ahead and do the best he could like a member of a good baseball team or orchestra. Even 8B had it—the fact that it was based on an anti-school-bureaucracy ideology didn't affect that. What mattered was that by and large they agreed among themselves about what they were doing there.

The problem with 7H was they had no solidarity.

The problem with 9D was that they had rejected the ordinary avenues of activity which had been offered to them, but hadn't come up with any alternative of their own. In fairness to them, it didn't seem likely that the possibility of making up their own alternatives had been often granted them. No, they had been presented year after year with an offer of certain things to either do or not-do, which is alternative enough in itself. I remember reading, from some novel or other, about two kids talking about class, this last alternative wasn't being offered. What to do? I wish school would start, said one kid, so we'd have something to do. What would we do then, man? asked the other. Then we could cut school! said the first.

They could not-go. Not-do it. It was something. Now, in our class, this last alternative wasn't being offered. What to do? They had never gotten the idea that they might be doing something else and still call it school.

What did I want them to do? I wanted them to learn something about English, since that was what they were spozed to learn in my class, and specifically I wanted them to learn something about writing—how to say what they wanted on paper so that somebody else could read it. But that brought us back to what they wanted to say, or anyway what they wanted to say on paper. That ought to be written down instead of just talked about. In this respect the discussions, upon which I'd counted, were a failure; no one found it necessary to record his own or anyone else's thoughts.

The problem with 9D was to find out what they wanted done which needed the classroom, the school situation, to do, which couldn't be done otherwise. I was committed now to finding it. I couldn't change now, hand out the spellers, give out ditto sheets with sentences to copy or diagram and all that without probable open rebellion, besides which I didn't want to anyway.

Still, what to do? It was no problem, there in the post office as November ended, to come to this sort of conclusion about GW. It was something else to think what to do about it. How grant solidarity to 7H? How discover what 9D wanted to do? I was never able to think of anything there, away from the class, so in December back I came to GW exactly in the same shape as when I'd entered that fall except for all this meditation, going into the classroom Monday morning without a specific plan of action, idiotically confident that something would turn up, determined—since I apparently couldn't do otherwise—to wait and see.

(22) Welcome Back!

Monday morning 7B and 8B seemed the same. They had few comments to make about the past month except for a few kids who said they were glad to see me back and a few others who said they wished they could still have Mrs. A, whose name I've forgotten.

9D, however, greeted me with an indignant and sincere-sounding outcry. Mrs. A was a better teacher than I, she was a real teacher, I wasn't no real teacher, she really made them work, not just have them old discussions every day; no, man, they were learning spelling and sentences and all they was spozed to. Moreover she was strict and didn't allow fooling around—all in all they felt they'd been really getting somewhere. I looked in my grade book, up to now pretty empty of marks, and saw, sure enough, a whole string of grades after each name—mostly, however, F's and zeroes. Many of them had nothing but zeroes, which I took to mean they had been busy not-doing this important work. I pointed this out to the class, but it didn't matter. They had been back on familiar ground; strict teacher, no fooling around, no smart-off, no discussions about how bad school was, and plenty of work. That was, after all, what school was and they were in favor of it.

7H was in a similar temper. They too had tales of plenty of real work, strict discipline, no talking, no gum, reading aloud every day, everybody—and then they came out with a long list of all of them who had been sent to the office for talking or chewing gum or refusing to read or laughing or getting mad at the teacher. Mrs. A gave them work on the board every day, they screamed, and she made them keep a notebook with all this work in it and they were spozed to bring it every day to work in and get graded on it. That was what real teachers did, they told me. I asked to see some of the notebooks; naturally no one had one. What about that? I asked. No use. She made us keep them notebooks, they all shouted. The fact that no one had kept or was keeping them notebooks didn't enter into it.

There were some more important changes. For one thing, John Banks was gone. Where? No one knew. Without him life in 8B was simpler, and I was happy about it. Also Virgil was gone from 7H. Everyone knew where he was—in Juvi, of course, for setting fire to several large garbage cans in the halls during one of the periods when he'd run out of class. I was pleased that he hadn't done it while I was there; he'd stopped running out of class after the first day anyway, presumably because we offered enough uproar and excitement right there to keep him content. He never came back to GW from Juvi, or at least I never saw him; there was talk that he'd been transferred to another school, but I don't really know. One of the Oriental kids was gone from 8B also; the kids said he went to Japan. This changed my statistics, but wasn't otherwise significant.

A big change was that everyone had them spellers. May showed hers off triumphantly. Most of the spellers in 9D were empty of writing—all that copying of words and alphabetizing and putting in lines between syllables hadn't actually been done except by May, Josephine and Geraldine. Theirs were all filled out to date, but were also all wrong. 7H had spellers too, but after the first victorious outcry their tone changed and they issued a complaint about them. For while Mrs. A was a great teacher, for evidence of which they had their nonexistent notebooks and blank spellers, she had made a serious mistake; the spellers were second- and third-grade spellers. We in the seventh grade, Mr. Hern-don! She give us the wrong spellers!

The state spellers tried to keep grade level a secret; they didn't say seventh grade or second grade anywhere on them, to keep the kids unaware of the fact they were working below (or above) grade level. What they did have was a number of dots, near the top, perhaps so the teacher could tell what grade level they were—seven dots for seventh grade, two dots for second grade. It didn't take long for the slowest kid to figure out this system.

7H raised hell with me about the second- and third-grade spellers. They needed seventh-grade spellers. They'd already had them second- and third-grade spellers for a number of years, they pointed out with some justification; they'd already not-done them a few times.

Hell, I thought; it didn't seem very important to me all of a sudden, and I went over and grabbed a stack of seventh-grade spellers from the shelf and passed them out. Everyone was delirious. The holidays were only a couple of weeks off, and I told them it was a Christmas present.

It was true the second- and third-grade spellers were of no use to them. What they needed was official spellers with seven big dots on them, to carry outside on the school grounds and home with them to prove they were too in seventh grade. I gave out a bunch of homework in spelling and ordered everyone to take the spellers home that very night to do the homework in; everyone carried those spellers home and back again every day from then on, until they were lost or swiped. I was, if not a real teacher like Mrs. A, at least a good guy again, and that was something. We were back to normal, ready to go.

(23) Mrs. A's Advice

In my free period that first day back I conferred with Mrs. A, who was sticking around to let me know what she'd been doing. She was an extremely attractive woman, perhaps thirty, well-dressed, light-colored, her hair nicely waved and under control; everything else was pretty well under control too, as I discovered. She told me, although not in so many words, that my classes had been a mess when she took over, that she considered them well on their way to straightening up after a month with her, and that it was now up to me to keep them that way. She got this across to me very nicely in the kind but firm manner some people have with training animals.

She advised me to figure out a regular and consistent plan of work, or simply to accept the one she had devised, and see to it that the students did this, or if not that they at least did nothing else during the period. I should grade all papers immediately and hand them back so that students who did the work could see their rewards promptly.

It was important, she said, to get them into the proper mood for schoolwork as soon as they entered the room. In particular, avoid beginning the period by talking to them, explaining, or lecturing, which they would not listen to and which only encouraged them to start talking themselves. She believed that I talked to the class too much anyway—there was no point in their expressing opinions about things they knew nothing about. Let them learn something first, she said, and then they might have something to say.

The best method for getting them in order was to have a paragraph written out on the board when they entered, and get them in the habit of copying this paragraph in their notebooks immediately they sat down, giving a time limit for its completion, erasing the paragraph when the time was up, and grading the notebooks frequently. Copying was something they could all do without further explanation from me; it got them in the mood for schoolwork, quiet, their materials ready, all set for the day's lesson, whatever it was.

I didn't have a lot to say to this advice. In the face of the nonexistent notebooks and the unused or all-wrong spellers, the list of those trooping down to the office for misbehavior, I couldn't see that the regimen had been a great success. In any case, the advice wasn't new. I'd been getting the same advice since September, especially the part about the paragraph. Perhaps after a year or so of this it might work; I didn't think so, but it didn't matter either. I knew damn well that they'd been getting this treatment for the past six years, that during this time they'd learned practically nothing about the "skills" this type of order was spozed to produce—no adverbs, not how to spell, no punctuation, not adding, subtracting, multiplying or dividing; many hadn't even learned how to read. I couldn't see my way had been a great success either—in fact, I didn't know what my way was—but the other was a failure and was going to be a failure. I couldn't see any reason to keep on doing it. I really couldn't.

I didn't say any of this to her. After all, she began to tell me about her own life; how she'd taught for five years, then had kids, stayed at home until the kids were in school, and was now coming back into the profession. She had a job for next year, full-time, for the district. She thought that what these kids needed was to learn to conform to the ordinary standards of American society, morals, and language. She also thought that too many teachers, faced with these children—we ignored The Word—just gave up on them, considered them hopeless, wouldn't give them a chance.

It wasn't surprising that we had so little to say to each other. She believed my classes were a mess because I was white and they were Negro kids and so I thought they weren't worth making an effort for. I thought she was working hard to help them in a way that hadn't ever helped them, wouldn't help them in the future, and was in fact cementing them into failure, rebellion or apathy. She thought I couldn't imagine them ever being tolerable students or responsible citizens. I thought that she, a middle-class Negro woman in a lamb's-wool sweater, had less contact with these students than I, knew less about them, mistrusted them more, thought less of their capabilities, and disliked them, as they were now, utterly.

(24) Other Things

During the short weeks before Christmas vacation I began to collect materials for what I hoped was an onslaught against 9D and 7H, but otherwise I simply let them follow Mrs. A's guide for hard work and success—assignments in the books, them spellers, homework, the notebooks and no discussions. Since Mrs. A wasn't really there, they continued to discuss and criticize as usual, but I didn't participate. Very little that happened now was going to count after Christmas, I reasoned, and I was trying to think. When my opinion on some crucial matter was requested I declined to answer; you guys are spozed to be doing all that real schoolwork, I told them, not just talking.

I kept casing mail at the post office after school, sometimes until midnight. When vacation started I worked eight or ten hours, into the early morning, until Christmas Eve, and we came close to breaking even financially.

After Christmas Skates came over a couple of times to visit. Skates, who was completely critical of every aspect of modern life, made exceptions for my wife Fran and my son Jay, who was about a year and a half. The evenings then were foggy, wet and cold, and Fran had generally made thick pea soup with ham and bacon and sausage floating in it, or perhaps stew with green onions and new potatoes and carrots, green peas, wine, rose-

mary and thyme or dill. You could see Skates's eye cloud over
and his revolutionist's soul relax, eating the soup or stew with
hot bread, watching the child play. How can the kid be so
beautiful? Skates would yell between mouthfuls. And your wife,
Jim! How could you get such a wife! You couldn't have done
better, he'd tell me over and over again during those evenings.
You couldn't have done better!

Later he always wanted to question Fran about her own
childhood. She was Indian, had grown up on a farm in North
Carolina where her father grew tobacco, and the group of
Indians around there were supposed to be the descendants of
both the Indians and the settlers of Roanoke Island, Raleigh's
mysterious colony.

He came over a number of times, then and later, and
soon had heard most of the stories. Still, whenever he came
he wanted to hear them over again. He wanted to hear about
how that town had triple segregation, three schools, white,
Negro, and Indian, about the Indian college that the whites
wanted to get into but weren't (yet) accepted in, about the
time the Klan came to town and the Indians all got their
rifles and met them in a field, about when the Gypsies came to
town, about when the anthropologists came to town, about the
famous outlaw Lowry. These are other things, Jim! he'd yell
over at me, interrupting some narrative. Other things to hear!
You couldn't have done better!

Sometimes he'd ask Fran, Well, what do you think about old
GW school? And she would answer something to the effect that
it sounded dreadful enough, all right, but that principally she
was afraid it was driving me nuts. Think of other things, Jim! he
would advise me. And then, turning to Fran, briefly his old
savage self, that lousy Grissum, that hatchet man, that rat! But
he's doing you a favor, Fran! He's railroading your husband out
of there! Believe me, it's a favor! A gift!

I was always astounded at this kind of talk. I couldn't see
that I was going nuts. I couldn't see that Grissum was railroading me. How was I nuts? What was Grissum doing to me? I
didn't worry about it though, and the conversation always
turned to other things.

(25) Carrots—Mrs. X's Advice

Two days after vacation I received a note from the secretary that Mrs. X (another name I don't remember) was coming down to talk to me. Mrs. X was the District Language and Social Studies consultant for GW.

Mrs. X didn't visit my classes. She met me in the teachers' room during my free period and opened the conversation by telling me that she came, as she did with all the new teachers, to offer any help or advice she could.

This Mrs. X was white, elderly, tall, stringy, wore a print dress—the very picture, I must say, of the old-lady school-teacher. She asked me if I had any problems I cared to mention. Did I? I began to outline them—9D's apathy, 7H's conglomeration of inabilities. I raced enthusiastically into a point-by-point description of the problems of 7H for a starter; I considered myself something of an expert on the subject. I spoke as if we two were going to reform the entire system, then and there.

Before I'd gotten fairly started, she interrupted. Now, we all have our problems, she said, and sometimes we're tempted to consider our own problems as being unique. But with *these* children (leaving out The Word, as usual) I've found that a simpler, more direct approach works best. I feel already that you may be making it all too complicated for yourself. In my experience, the best advice I can give you beginning teachers is, hold out a carrot.

A carrot? I didn't get it.

You know, she said brightly, the carrot, or perhaps we should say a sugar cube. If you want the goat to pull the cart, but he doesn't want to, you hold a carrot out in front of him. He tries to reach the carrot because he does want it. In doing so he pulls the cart. *If,* she said with a kind of wink, *if* you've attached the carrot to the cart.

I must have seemed a little stupid to her. Seeing that I just sat there, she tried to explain. Teaching these children is like training animals. For each task you want them to do, you must offer them a carrot.

You mean, I finally said, you try to get the goat to pull the cart without his realizing it. That is, the goat actually does what you want him to do, but all the time he thinks he's just trying to get that carrot. He doesn't realize he's pulling the cart. Not only that, but pulling the cart isn't something that any goat, any normal goat, ever wants to do, but . . .

I think you're trying to make it complicated again, she said, frowning.

You mean, I tried again, to get the student to do the assignment because of some reward he's going to get, not because he realizes that the assignment is valuable or interesting to him. You mean, the assignment itself can't be the carrot . . .

She felt happier. That's it, she said. Of course the reward must vary. There are individual differences as we know. A carrot for one, a sugar cube for another.

Mercifully the bell rang. Mrs. X went back to her desk in the district office, downtown. I sneaked a quick smoke, my mind filled with carrots and outrage, and arrived upstairs a bit late to greet 9D.

(26) Projection—Mr. Grisson's Advice

The next day I was invited, during my free period, to Mr. Grisson's office for a talk. As it turned out, that was normal procedure after a visit from the consultant. I was still outraged about them carrots and also I was tired of taking up my free time—during which I planned to drink coffee and smoke cigarettes—with substitutes and consultants. I believe I had some idea that Grissum and I, both being involved in the "real" situation, would soon settle these damn people.

So when he asked me how things went with Mrs. X, I was ready. I stated that she was hardly a person to be advising beginning teachers, seeing as how she thought that teaching kids was about the same as training a dog to play dead. He didn't seem disturbed. Instead, as I paused for breath, he said, I believe your problem is one of projection. You are not projecting.

Again I didn't get it.

Your voice, he said; projection, like an actor, or a good officer. The tone of command. Men, or children, hearing the voice properly projected, stop, pay attention, and tend to do what the voice says. Your voice hasn't that effect. You find yourself, for instance, shouting to get their attention.

That was the first I knew that he had any idea what went on

in my room. Well, I said, I more or less think that the reason I shout is because they're all talking at once and otherwise they wouldn't hear me.

He shook his head. That's not the point. The point is to have them firmly in control by your voice as soon as they enter. Before they ever get into that state. Now, I'm going to arrange for you to have voice lessons. You'll be able to take them here, at the school, during your free period. You'll find it to be of great value, wherever you go and whatever you do.

Fine, I said, not knowing what else to say. I was rather astounded. I didn't have the slightest idea what he was talking about; also, I'd momentarily forgotten about my free period.

It's an excellent experience, he said. You'll be notified when the program starts.

The interview was clearly over. Still, I didn't feel we understood each other. Voice lessons were OK, but I had something else to say.

Mr. Grisson, I said, I'm sure voice lessons will be of value (I wasn't sure), but the thing is, I don't feel the problem is that I can't get them under control. I've had quite a bit of advice on that subject and I'm sure it's not very difficult to do that. The thing is, *I* don't want to *get them* under control. I want them to see some reason for getting *themselves* under control.

He began to look at me intently. I rushed on. It seemed to me, I told him, that they'd been having this firm control for years now, and it hadn't worked. They still hadn't seen any advantage in self-control, so obviously it hadn't worked!

Your description is correct, he said, but your conclusions, as I interpret them, are wrong. For if they've not yet learned self-control, then they must be controlled until they do learn it. You are the person to do that. It does them no good to be out of control, and it is dangerous. It is dangerous to them, and to the orderly running of the unit, the school.

He was intent and serious; he had a few things to say himself, apparently.

History shows, he said, that democracy is only granted to

those populations who can manage their own affairs, who can do what is necessary without being forced to. The moment they no longer can, a leader, a monarch, even a dictator, takes over and orders them to do what they cannot make themselves do. That may be unpleasant for them, but it is inevitable.

(27) Comes the Revolution—Skates's Advice

In between his threatening the traffic going both ways and his complaints about his affairs and landlady, I was able to tell Skates about all the advice I was receiving.

He was appropriately indignant. This would never happen in Chicago! he told me. That's your free time! You ought to get double time to have to hear that bullshit during your free period! Screw them! Be happy if you get fired.

But, man! I said, feeling he wasn't getting the point. How can you call that teaching? How can I have kids copy stuff off the board who can't read their own names? Why should I give out assignments to kids who don't see any reason to do anything, let alone those assignments? And those carrots! What kind of carrot? Let alone the principle of the thing, just leave that part aside for a minute, these kids won't go for those phony rewards anyway! They know that's all crap, those A's, stars, all that.

Surprisingly, Skates disagreed. No they don't, he said. They don't know anything, not even that. This is capitalism, don't you understand? Each one thinks he'll get ahead of the next kid, this time! I tell my kids, Do this assignment and you'll get an A, you can have a talent show, you can goof off the whole last week of school! You think they don't do it? They do it! And as long as they do it, they're leaving my ass alone. They aren't screaming and hollering about their goddam tennis or their lousy paper!

Teaching? Hell no, it ain't teaching! What do you expect? I'm telling you that under capitalism, under this lousy, stinking social system, those kids are fucked, and no one knows it better than they do. Under capitalism all they can do is try to get ahead of the next kid, and they do it, they will! The best they can think of to do, when they really try, is to copy the pitiful cringing white petty bourgeoisie.

You've got to wait, Jim! You got to wait for the revolution! Socialism! This isn't a school! It's a place where those kids can find out once and for all what they're up against, where the ruling class says in no uncertain terms to them, Forget you! You ain't going nowhere! Go on and learn to tap-dance or be a jitney girl, because you ain't going nowhere.

But you, Jim, you got to live. You got your wife—your wife, Jim, who makes that soup on those cold evenings, that beautiful kid. You got to put those paragraphs on the board for them to copy as long as they'll still do it. You've got no real union here, you're alone in there, between the victims and the exploiters.
. . .

I could never tell if Skates was serious about the revolution or not. In the end I thought he had believed in it once, didn't see any chance for it now, but continued talking in terms of it anyway. It was, in a sense, a useful way of interpreting things. I asked him if he put those paragraphs on the board, and he said he damn well did. I asked him if it worked, and he said it did, at least for about the first ten or fifteen minutes. After that, he said, calming down, some of them will go on and work at something and I can play with the rest. I figure I owe them that much.

(28) Mrs. Y—The End of Advice

Skates analyzed my situation for me: the sub (Mrs. A) had said I was incompetent, and the consultant (Mrs. X) had come down to talk to me. Neither she nor Grissum had been satisfied; they couldn't quite decide, so the language supervisor (Mrs. Y) arrived in a couple more days to observe me and my classes. It was a catastrophe.

Mrs. Y arrived in the afternoon, just in the middle of 7B's editing period—the third stage of their composition unit. The stories had already been written and read aloud, and now had been passed out to other kids for them to edit—make corrections, remarks, suggestions—and give back to the writers. It was work everyone liked; they corrected with crusading zeal and commented freely and at length on the cover sheets I gave them. It was the only time in the whole day when I really knew what we were doing.

Mrs. Y sat in the back of the room, watching, I suppose, the kids talking back and forth about the papers and writing on them and showing what they'd written to everyone else, and observing me walking around, looking at the work, making a mark here and there, talking to a kid—the period passed quickly. Near the end some of them read the comments which had been made on their work and there was a lot of spirited arguing back and forth. Then the bell rang, and I was hoping she would go on back downtown, but no luck. She stayed there in the back of the room, nodded to me, said nothing, didn't ask what the kids had been doing; 8B entered, and we opened up with a dull fifteen minutes of instruction on how to use quotation marks. I demonstrated on the board, explained, referred to pages in the book. 8B couldn't have been less interested, but the presence of Mrs. Y—whom they didn't know—inspired them to the kind of phony eagerness they reserved for visits from important people like Grissum or Miss Bentley. Even that wore off before the period was half over, but by that time I had assigned them a bunch of sentences to punctuate with these same quotation marks, so they had to make a show out of that too, writing furiously. By the time that wore off, the period was over. I felt uncomfortable with Mrs. Y in the room, just sitting there. I knew she was there to judge my work, and, considering that I didn't know what I was doing, I wished they could have waited awhile. Not yet! I wanted to say; come around later when I've got it all figured out! Still I couldn't see that it had gone badly at all. 7B had been at their best—bright, witty and peaceable, doing something they liked to do, and 8B had conned themselves into a semblance of respectability. Surely she'll go on back now, I thought, but someone must have tipped her off—she was determined to stick around and have a look at 7H.

They came hooting up the stairs as usual, their day almost over, one more crazy period. They flung themselves into the room shouting information, what Roy did in Mr. Brook's room and what Mr. Brooks say, what Alexandra say then and so Mr. Brooks he say it ain't no business of Alexandra's . . . the usual jubilant five minutes, ending up normally with the question: What we going to do today, Mr. Herndon?

I had already given that question some thought, in view of Mrs. Y. For the first time I wished old Virgil was back so we could put on our reading groups which looked so good to Harvey. On the other hand I'd been thinking that it was about time to start them up again, choose some new leaders to take

Virgil's place . . . why not? I thought. After all, it was about all we had to show Mrs. Y. So I decided to try it with Judy and Wade, a big kid who read pretty well and who didn't have any outstanding quarrels with anyone; after some shouting to get everyone in seats and quiet, I announced we were going to have reading groups. Immediately a chorus of yells went up, mostly to the point of who was going to be the leader of the other group? Each one suggested himself, and each suggestion met with loud and derogatory comment. I proposed Wade. General outrage at my stupidity. What? Wade? That watermelon-headed . . . and so on. Wade got mad then, of course, and rose up, threatening to whip someone's black ass, and inevitably then proud Alexandra took it upon herself to call Wade down. But poor Wade, like everyone else there, was afraid of Alexandra so he quickly discovered he was mad at Harvey and called *him* down so it would seem like he just didn't have time for Alexandra. Everyone was standing now, rushing around to confront someone else or yelling across the room; Roy, out of everyone's league as far as fighting was concerned, dashing up to me to laugh and laugh—it was a madhouse.

Still, we'd had uproars before. We had them every time some new arrangement had to be made in the class. (We had them other times, too, for other reasons or for no reason as far as I knew, but this kind was predictable. I should have thought of it, in view of Mrs. Y.) The uproar meant simply that they weren't sure what was going to happen, that as soon as it was possible to be heard I would have to explain it to them while they examined the proposition from every angle for hidden dangers and traps, and then we would go ahead and try to do it or else abandon it if it proved too risky. I mean to say I was used to it, and although Mrs. Y was still there in the back of my mind, I thought she'd see what the panic was all about and it might even be a useful demonstration. I got ready to begin cooling everyone off, thinking that perhaps we should have two, maybe three more reading leaders which would take the pressure off of Wade and the group too, planning how to explain it for all of us. I moved over to deal with Alexandra first, who by this time was angrily claiming that Wade was trying to start a fight with her so's she would get in trouble and how she didn't let nobody pick on her . . . but all of a sudden everyone shut up and I looked around and saw that Mrs. Y was standing there in front of the class.

In all my life, said Mrs. Y, I have never seen such a rude, disorderly, disgraceful class!

(29) Grissum Steps In

It was in the kids' language that Mr. Grisson's name always came out Grissum. They didn't intend to ridicule him; it just came out that way. In time many of the teachers could be heard saying Grissum too, and looking back at these pages, I find it written that way more than once. Around GW it just seemed to fit.

He called me into his office the day after Mrs. Y's visit. Her moral lecture to 7H about courtesy and behavior had not been a success, a fact which both surprised and angered her. It had probably always worked for her—meaning that the kids, whatever kids, had lowered their heads and looked ashamed and shut up while being lectured. It probably hadn't made anyone more courteous in the long run, as Mrs. Z, for one, would have known.

Anyway, 7H didn't take to head-lowering. They had started in immediately to argue with her. They weren't doing anything wrong, they interrupted her to say, Why was she coming into their room talking like that? This Mr. Hern-don's class, it ain't yours! How come you spozed to be here telling us what to do?

It got worse and worse. Mrs. Y couldn't believe her ears. I sat down; it was all hers. Harvey stood up and said indignantly, We trying to get our reading groups and you won't let us do it!

Alexandra got mad and stood up too and yelled that no one was going to tell her that she wasn't nice, whereupon Roy yelled out that Alexandra wasn't nice nor her mama either and everyone else laughed and Mrs. Y screeched out that she'd never been so insulted in her entire life, and left.

Mr. Grisson wanted to know if I thought it correct that my class should be allowed to insult a visitor. No, I didn't, I said. On the other hand, I said, no one had insulted her at all until she got up and called the class rude. Since she'd decided to take charge of the class, I figured she wanted to go ahead and handle it.

He considered that. Then he said, Why do you suppose she decided to take over your class?

Well, from what she said, she thought they were acting badly and wanted to straighten them out. I feel she should have left them alone.

I went on to tell him what we'd been doing, explained that the uproar was caused by the approach of a new arrangement and so on.

Did you appoint a reading leader? he asked.

Yeah, I said, I suggested a kid.

And do you think the students were going to be able to pick out a better person to be leader?

No, I admitted that Wade was probably the best one. I tried to explain that we would have ended up with Wade anyway, tried hurriedly to mention 7H's fears about reading, reading leaders, but time had run out. He told me to expect him today, last period.

The class needs a firm reprimand for yesterday's actions, he said, and obviously he, not I, was the person to accomplish that. Also, he added, that class is going to be here, all together, all this year. I think it best they understand once and for all how they are to behave. And you yourself will be able to see an excellent method for insuring that.

Last period that day 7H piled up the stairs, but stopped short when they saw Grissum standing by the door. We all went into the room; the kids sat down and I took up a position over by the windows. Grissum stood in front of the class, erect, looking straight ahead—we all waited until the bell rang. At that, Grissum told them in a few short sentences that they had misbehaved, explained the high status of the visitor, described her shock. He wondered if they desired it to be said downtown that GW was a school where visitors hated to come, for fear of being insulted.

Then he told them that Mr. Herndon would pass out paper— I went over to get it—and that they were to wait in silence while he wrote something on the board. While he wrote, I passed out the sheets. The kids were all saying, Thank you, Mr. Herndon, in meek voices, trying to make things right. Grissum finished writing and turned around. He began by saying that what he'd written was a contract. Do you know what a contract is? He told them briefly that it meant that both sides agreed to do certain things, that neither side was to break faith, and then he told them to copy the paragraph on the paper I'd handed out.

The paragraph itself said something about how I the under-signed promise to behave properly and according to the stand-ards of GW at all times, etc. It didn't say what Grissum or GW was promising to do for them. I stood around, feeling vaguely as if I should be copying it down too. Grissum stood erect and motionless in his light gray suit. No one said anything. It lasted about fifteen minutes—it took a long time for 7H to draw those words on that paper, for that was what most of them had to do, of course, draw those words, leave spaces, connect those letters, space, draw some more.

Finally Grissum told them to sign their names at the bottom. They all did. Then he went to each kid and collected his contract, shaking each one's hand as he did so. Then, all done, he told them they'd shaken hands on the bargain, they'd made an agreement, and he was going to keep those contracts in his office for the rest of the year. He knew no one there was going to break his contract. Am I right? he asked them. Yes, Mr. Grissum, we all agreed. Good, he said firmly, and off he went.

There were about ten minutes left in the period, during which all hell broke loose.

(30) Action Now!

So the advice of the sub, the visits of Mrs. X and Mrs. Y and Grissum's demonstration didn't do any good. If that was all they had to say, I figured I was on my own.

Also I decided not to wait for the revolution. Perhaps that was because I couldn't see that anyone was going to make one very soon, at least none that would do The Tribe any good—in fact I thought that anything like that was going to have to come from The Tribe itself. I wanted that revolution now, in my classroom—by which I simply mean, as before, solidarity as a class for 7H and the figuring out of their own possibilities and desires for 9D. I didn't know what any of this would mean for their futures, for the community, for socialism, for history. . . . I'm trying to make it clear that I was concerned for them as they were, and where they were, now, in my class. That took care of the paragraphs and the contracts too, whose purpose as far as I could see was to keep The Tribe from coming to their revolution.

After the visits and advice, I was able to get going. I stopped trying to "figure out" methods that were foolproof or "the best" . . . and I simply started in with everything it had occurred to me to try out.

The first thing I did was to try unashamedly to unload Roy

onto my Irish FTA comrade in Reading Improvement, but that
was no go. He argued (correctly) that R.I. was meant to
improve reading, not teach it from scratch; also he'd heard
about Roy and obviously wanted no part of him. So I got hold
of the English Department chairman, another attractive and
freckle-faced Negro woman, and asked for her help with my
nonreaders; she agreed to take them individually during eighth
period, when her time was free to deal with various problems,
among which presumably Roy *et al.* could be included. She told
me a few things about kids' problems with peer-group conflicts,
and how often they would learn better in a one-to-one relationship.

We finally decided on three new group leaders in 7H, among
whom one was Wade. The school equipment included a tape
recorder which no one was using, so we kept it. None of the
three new leaders was much more skillful than the members of
their groups and so the work of the groups went on differently
than it had with Virgil and Judy—so differently that Judy didn't
fit in as a leader any more. So I took her off that job and made
her a kind of roving consultant, an expert, since she was the
only one who really knew anything and also since she had
become an intolerable bully in her group. She now roamed
around snooping at flash cards and words and correcting people
mercilessly, but since she had to take care of the whole class she
was spread a bit thin and everyone was able to take it. She was
also official speller to the class, in case anyone really wanted to
spell something; some days were full of arbitrary requests which
kept her busy and happy at the board and with the dictionary.

In 9D I announced that we would continue to have regular
work with the spellers and the language book. This plan was
rejected loudly by most, with arguing and threats of rebellion.
That sort of thing was OK for Mrs. A who was a real teacher,
but not for me. So I announced that this "regular" work would
be voluntary, but it would be offered. We would change seating
arrangements too, I said, so that those who wanted to try to
learn this work could be together. This was acclaimed by all as
fair. May and friends formed the obvious nucleus for the group,

and several kids, wavering, joined them. The three C's stayed at the table. The rest of the class solidified itself on the other side of the room around Verna, whose back was turned as it had been since my announcement. We began the usual discussions about how this would affect everyone; I required that enough order be maintained to allow the "regulars" (as they were already being called) to do their studious work. There was a good ·deal of questioning to see if I really meant it—the part about *voluntary,* that is; when that was established they were enthusiastic about ground rules for my behavior and theirs, settling in the main for the system that I was to leave the non-regulars strictly alone, not "bothering" them, as long as they weren't breaking any "school rules." I did point out that most of them were breaking several school rules all the time, especially the ones involving eating, chewing, cosmetics (applying in class), combs (combing hair in class), shoes (changing in class), and transistors (playing in class). That was judged beside the point; they meant breaking them badly or defiantly— playing the transistors loudly, throwing the food and that kind of thing.

I also signed up for library hours for both 7H and 9D at regular periods at least once a week. Both classes, long rejected from the library, were astonished and exuberant. The librarian was horrified. She was a young Italian girl, rather prim, who believed that the only purpose of the school library was for kids to come in, get books and either take them out immediately or else sit down there immediately and begin to read them. Other permitted activities were (1) looking through the card file, (2) asking the librarian questions about where to find things, where-upon she directed them to the card file, and (3) copying sections out of the encyclopedia, an activity which was called "research." Talking, even whispering, was not a permitted activity, since the kids were supposed to "learn how to behave in the public libraries," as if no one ever talked in a public library.

Most of these activities worked out about as expected. Roy had gone out to see Mrs. Robbins (the chairman) first—a candidate, so I stated, for an experiment in reading. He left grinning, accompanied by the outraged cries of 7H to the effect of why didn't I pick them? Roy returned angrily at the end of the period, threatened several kids and finally yelled that that teacher was trying to make him do that kindergarten stuff. He brought a note with him, quite long; its theme, briefly, was that Roy was impossible (he wouldn't sit down, he wouldn't stop laughing, she was afraid of him) and that it was an inefficient use of teacher time (hers) which should go to help those students who had both the desire and the potential for learning. So the next day I sent Vincent; he lasted two periods but then she met me at lunchtime saying that Vincent's "mental problem —his poor eyes!" made him impossible to teach also, meek and mild as he undoubtedly was. I told Vincent the experiment was over, and fired off Alexandra the next day. I guess Alexandra had figured out that nonreading was the actual subject of this experiment, for she was back in about fifteen minutes telling me that she didn't allow nobody to treat her like that! Mrs. Robbins told me the next day that Alexandra had stomped in and told her without being asked that she did so already know how to read and threatened her with her mama, and apparently Mrs. Robbins didn't allow nobody to treat *her* like that either. Besides, Mrs. Robbins told me, she was going to be working now with "a group of ninth-grade (A) girls who were going to put out the Yearbook" and expected her eighth-period time would be pretty much required by them. She informed me too that with kids like Roy and Alexandra, often a one-to-one basis amounted to pampering, and it was perhaps more necessary that they work on adjustment to their peer-group situation. Anyway their records didn't indicate that they were nonreaders, and was I sure? I told her I'd look into it; Harvey never got his turn at the big experiment.

The tape recorder was something of a success with 7H. Several of the kids got proficient at running it, for one thing. We used it once a week all by itself, with the condition that anyone who could or would read something out of our collection of books, or else read something they'd written themselves, would be recorded and played back. It worked out, of course, that many kids just got up and orated into it, but after the first few times there was little of that; group readings were popular after awhile, several kids taking a story and splitting it up, and when we got through an entire story we were able to play it back with pretty great admiration for ourselves. Roy and Harvey almost always had something perfectly memorized for the occasion and recited brilliantly, holding the book before them in a professional manner. I couldn't see that it did any harm, and, oddly enough, it didn't affect those who could read. They never memorized anything themselves, but kept on stumbling laboriously through unfamiliar passages, enduring the transparent mockery of Roy. Vincent was allowed to recite on occasion without holding the book; we were sympathetic with his problem. Alexandra alone would never read or speak even her name into the machine, suspicious, perhaps, that some trap was concealed in it. During recording days she could be heard sometimes muttering warnings against the machine from the back of the room.

We also used the recorder on spot occasions to tape sessions with the reading groups. Listening to these later, I was always amazed at the interminable personal argument, threat and counterthreat which went on over the simplest matters. For it can't be assumed that with the groups arranged again, the recorder, etc., the class now went smoothly. We now had a number of things going in the room—the groups were expanded to include spelling and writing groups, where the kids tried to use their (second- and third-grade) spellers, the leaders asking words, or having the kids make up sentences from the words, or the groups could choose from a selection of games like simple Scrabble, or spin-the-pointer games where they had to pick a card and follow printed instructions. (The school had a number of these for use on rainy days when kids had to stay inside at lunch, and 7H had brought some of their own too.) We had our library periods, our films (shortly after this time). Still, most of the time each period was spent arguing about what they were going to do or weren't; if they were, then who was going to do it;

battling each other about their tennis, or about whose fault it was that Mr. Brooks was coming to keep them. Each school day seemed to furnish them with enough material for a lifetime's complaint, and they were, most times, unable to see each other as anything but potential and momentary allies or enemies.

9D's problem didn't change either; we now had some activity going on besides the interminable discussion, but only in addition to it, not instead of it. Here I should say that my advisers were all correct in their feeling (the feeling I'm sure lay behind all their advice) that once a class sees that you are really going to discuss their possible activities with them, really delegate or even give up all this wonderful authority the school system has endowed you with, once you allow kids in a class to do only what they themselves want to do even if this doesn't happen to turn out to be what you want them to do—once this happens, you can't ever take charge and order them about again with any success. Many teachers who enter into this kind of thing with a class, by way of experiment—to see if it will work—suffer disappointment because of this fact. But that is because they've somehow been led to expect that a class of kids will, if left to make their own decisions, decide to do what the teacher planned to do—homework, read the text, do those sentences and exercises. The class won't. Why should it? Given a taste of something like that, they aren't likely to want to give it up very soon, seeing as how it is really a kind of freedom. These teachers then finally come to believe that it is simply a hindrance to instruction, to their method, and of course it is. For myself I didn't see it as hampering anything, since in itself it was my method as far as I had one. The only thing I had against it was that it was going too slowly (or possibly nowhere at all), it was a hell of a lot of work, nerve-racking, and, of course, too damn noisy.

But now at least we had a prearranged method of beginning class which, really, everyone could approve. I was to review yesterday's work with the regulars over by the windows, assign something else, explain the assignment, and help them to get started on the next leg of their long journey toward the land of private secretaries. There were some real advantages here. The main thing was that during this time no one could ask me some leading question, like: Mr. Herndon, if Lowell throw a apple at some girl out in the yard and say that Robert did it, and if the girl then come over and kick Robert, do Robert have the right to beat Lowell's fuzzy head off with a stick? That is, they could ask, and did, but they didn't have the right to ask, and I, on the other hand, did have the right to refuse to answer. The other advantage was of course that it satisfied the regulars, who after all had the right to do what they wanted also, even if that happened to be receiving instruction from me.

The regulars varied in number from day to day, although sometime during the year everyone joined it just to see how it was—everyone but Verna. The normal regular enrollment was from eight to ten, and of these some worked conscientiously every day at spellers, exercises, punctuation, paragraphs, *et al.;* they refused to get involved in anything "unofficial" or "creative"—they would write stories, for instance, if the book suggested they do so, but not otherwise. Some of the regulars sat there each day listening to assignment and explanation but didn't do any of the work. I didn't comment either way—about who worked, joined, didn't work. I felt I'd already given my opinion on its value and it was up to them.

The tape recorder, by the way, was of no interest to 9D, outside of a couple of kids who liked to fool with it and see how it worked. They weren't impressed with it and didn't need it. I tried, for instance, to get them interested in making up disc-jockey programs and recording them, with records, commercials, talk, etc., but they couldn't see it. If they wanted a disc-jockey program, they told me, all they had to do was to listen to their Japanese transistors; they weren't interested in pretending. It was the same story with classroom movies which 7H, above all, loved; 9D rejected them, didn't want to see them, didn't want to be interrupted by them.

9D was, by contrast, quite impressed with my proposed library period. As long as it lasted, it was the only time when they fell back into the usual school attitude—namely, that I, as teacher, was "taking them" somewhere. After the first few minutes of the first visit, when they saw clearly that the librarian was alarmed by them, they demanded their regular turn, and marched in like an invading army. They roamed through the place touching books, opening and closing catalog drawers, making sure everyone could see they were allowed the freedom of the place. These activities were of course within the scope of the librarian's approval, as they well knew, but the only trouble was that the goal of this activity—the finding of a book and sitting down to read it or copy it—was something they never did. After the first or second visit, it was clear that the only thing they liked to do in there was to sit or stand by the big front window and watch the streetcars, passersby, buses—and talk to each other about the sights. Naturally these two activities were forbidden on the grounds that they weren't what the library was for.

Interestingly enough, the regulars got into more trouble than anyone else; they wouldn't leave their various workbooks behind in class and had no time for anything so frivolous as browsing or "free reading," and of course working in textbooks or workbooks wasn't allowed in the library since that also wasn't what the library was for. The librarian was continually demanding that they stop working in these books, and the regulars kept on trying to tell her about their serious and compelling need to do it. I took them to the library for about five or six weeks before they regained their senses and refused to go, on the reasonable grounds that there wasn't anything there that they wanted to do. Two or three kids who actually wanted to check out books and read were sent regularly by me, subject to the librarian's approval, which worked out fine.

7H was, as usual, something else. They rushed on the library as if to devour it before it could get away. Every kid snatched as many books off the shelves as he could hold and hurried off with them to a table, sat, and angrily surrounded them with his arms against attack. They grabbed any kind of book—novels, science, encyclopedias, the bigger the better, rushed through the stack in about five minutes, and were up for another pile or else trying to take likely looking volumes from other kids' tables.

Unlike 9D, who all wanted to sit around one table together (forbidden), 7H each wanted a table to himself (also forbidden). The librarian was horrified. I didn't blame her. I was horrified myself, and I already knew them. She demanded their attention and obedience to library rules, but no one heard. What they were doing was vital, had to be done. She turned to me. Who were these kids? Could they read? Why did I bring them? She was really upset. This couldn't possibly go on; I was not to think of bringing them again. I tried to tell her that if they came regularly and got the idea that the books were always going to be there and they could always have a look at them, they might be able to settle down and take it a little easy. She didn't believe it, and I wasn't sure I did. I added, though, that they were all students at GW and ought to be allowed a chance at this privilege. We agreed finally to try it again. She was to look around for some books that they might actually be able to read when they came next time, which seemed a good idea, and I was really pleased and impressed with her that she even thought about allowing them back. Since it was the last period, we were able to make 7H stay around and help reshelve the books, and that made a good impression.

The next time we came down, she was all set with a lot of possible books—things from "easy reading" all the way down to absolute beginning books, the kind that are large and have pages made up of a big picture and a few words underneath, alphabet books, for instance. We were prepared and managed to get them seated before they got hopelessly lost in their lust for the research volumes. She started talking to them about these new books, and pulled them out of the shelves here and there, but of course 7H recognized them all as them kindergarten and baby books and who did she think they were? Finally released, they rushed as before for the heavy, thick, erudite-looking volumes and uproar followed. Fortunately the librarian, being a librarian, hadn't just put all those kindergarten books out by themselves on a table, but had painstakingly integrated them with the other fiction, or nonfiction, however it was. Therefore 7H, many of whom really wanted to have a look at them, was able to sneak these baby books out of the stacks and conceal them among their other tomes; during the period I could see quite a few kids staying in one place for awhile as they read about *Johnny and the Fire Engine,* behind a tall stack of the Junior Harvard Classics.

It is one of the greatest difficulties at a Junior High to find material for slow-reading kids to read. All the books written in simple enough language are always books for little kids; not only are these always identifiable as such and therefore beyond the pale, but they are also too childish in subject matter. It's been forgotten somehow along the way that slow readers aren't necessarily slow in other ways, aren't less grown-up than fast readers—in any case, they certainly aren't interested in the things first-graders are.

At GW there was the added difficulty that none of these books acknowledged anywhere within its covers the existence of Negroes or of a real lower class of any sort, and they often, even with their childishness, assumed a wealth of experience that The Tribe simply wasn't up to. One day in 7H, for example, I opened up a book to a picture of some people camping beside a lake in a tent.

Look at them crazy people, Roy roared out. They so poor they have to go live in a tent! There was some disbelief expressed at this shocking circumstance, and Harvey shouted out that they ain't crazy, them is Indians, that why they live in that tent! But everybody could see they weren't Indians at all, they didn't have the right clothes. Even 7B was upset by the idea, expressed in a story we read one day, that a kid their age might go all over town by himself and even get on a bus and go out of town to the airport and watch the planes take off—they thought that extremely farfetched and unrealistic.

In a way this very lack of experience—this common, ordinary American experience taken for granted by the writers of these books—helped us out for once. For 7H wasn't really bored by these childish books. Somehow they'd never gotten around to reading about *Johnny and the Fire-Engine,* or about *Cowboy Small, Captain Small,* or *Policeman Small,* and many of them were anxious to make up for lost time, their only problem being how to remain undetected while doing it. So after a few weeks I began to feel the library period was something of a success with them. True, Roy remained uncontrollable and had to be kicked out almost every time; others occasionally joined him, and it wasn't quite the studious, pleasant period we enjoyed with 7B.

Just how unlike that it was became clear to me suddenly one period when Roy, who had been sent out in the hall, reappeared with Miss Bentley right behind him. She asked me why Roy was out in the hall, and I said it was just that he couldn't let the other kids alone and I'd sent him out there to cool off a bit. All the time she was looking around and I saw 7H through her eyes. There they were, sitting one to a table behind huge stacks of books, crouching down low with their big, bright preschool reading material, fussing at each other all the time, various kids squabbling over an impressive volume, standing, rushing to the shelves, staggering back with an armload. It occurred to me I'd been with 7H too long. I could see that this library period, which I'd just been thinking was a pretty successful one, appeared to Miss Bentley as a most disgusting spectacle, and indeed she asked me if I truly thought 7H needed to use the library. I said that I thought if they wanted to go, they should be taken even though I knew they had some trouble using the facilities properly, and she left.

The next day she saw me at lunch and talked to me about it. She told me that often teachers who thought they were providing some kind of equal opportunity were really just avoiding their responsibilities. I felt she thought I was taking them to the library in order to loaf, to get the librarian to help me control them, to let the kids goof off. I feel, she said, that groups should use facilities when they are ready to do so properly. If they are not, they do not raise themselves up to the level of the majority, but pull the majority down to their level. And that, at GW, would be most unfortunate indeed.

She left it at that. Committed, we rolled in and out of the library, regulars and nonregulars, readers and nonreaders, going somewhere, I hoped, not yet convinced that that somewhere was straight up the creek.

(31) Honorable Mention

During Christmas vacation I had come across Paul Roberts'
book *Patterns of English,* the first (and at that time, the only)
high school English text based on modern linguistics or structural grammar. I knew little about linguistics and so learned a
good deal myself from it, but what impressed me about it was
that the exercises for the students to do seemed at one and the
same time very practical and extremely interesting. I immediately tried them out on 7B when I came back, and they were a
great success.

Very briefly, the idea was to teach kids the various different
kinds of words (the "parts of speech") by the way in which
they occurred in sentences—within the sentence structure—
instead of according to the meaning of the word. That is, a word
wasn't to be called a noun because it was a person, place or
thing necessarily, but because it occurred in normal sentences in
a certain way. If you took the sentence "The——— is new,"
you could see that only certain words would fit that blank, and
those words we could call nouns or anything else; whatever they
meant, they still were the only kinds of words that would fit
there.

This seemed simple and interesting, and 7B was enthusiastic.
They learned the various "patterns" easily, and by the time the

year was over had gone through about half the book, which was meant for upper-grade high-school kids. I began now to try it out with 9D and 7H and the results were, relatively, quite as good. The regulars in 9D disapproved because it wasn't in their book, but they did it anyway because I told them they'd get graded on it. I was allowed to make this kind of statement to the regulars. We did these patterns once a week and on that day almost everyone became a regular. They enjoyed making up huge lists of words that would fit certain patterns, and became fairly sure of themselves when it came to naming the patterns. The opposite exercise, that of taking a nonsense sentence and trying to figure out which words were nouns, adjectives, etc., was a great favorite; it had all the virtues, being new, fun and not difficult.

We did this once a week in 7H too; they particularly liked to take the simple patterns and provide rhyming words for them and would go so far as to write these down, many of them, and to comment on which rhyming words looked the same, which pairs didn't. Pretty soon I was able to get the group leaders to provide simple patterns and get some reponse from their group.

This is a plug for Roberts' book, then. Did I mention 8B? Well, 8B didn't care about patterns I must admit. But for 7B the work was stimulating and new and, I felt, more real (certainly more accurate) as a way of studying grammar. With 9D and 7H, it was the only thing I was able to point to as something I was teaching them, in the ordinary classroom sense, and I was happy about that.

(32) Melanie

I believe it was in the middle of February that we had a diversion in 7H in the form of a real, live, freckled, red-haired, white, Okie girl, who appeared in class one day, enlivened us for two weeks, and was gone. Her name was Melanie Franklin.

Melanie put everyone straight the first day. She announced that she would like to invite all the kids in the class home with her, but her Aunt didn't allow no niggers in the house. No *colored,* she amended, and made it clear that it was the aunt who put it that way: no *niggers.*

Oddly enough, this didn't bother anyone in 7H. In the first place Melanie spent most of her time flirting and carrying on with all the boys in the class and when I drove up in the mornings I always saw her perched up on the fireplug on the corner surrounded by boys, talking and laughing as they all showed off. Second, she was friendly with the girls; Alexandra took a great liking to her and was even rather sad, I thought, when Melanie left.

The great revelation was that Melanie, although white as they come, wasn't any smarter than the rest of 7H. She could read a little, but not as much as Wade, let alone Judy. She opened up a world of possibilities to 7H. She talked freely about her aunt's many "uncles," how often they came around, what they did, how long they stayed, and she told long stories of her rambles around the town which always seemed to end up in the bus station downtown—a long way from GW, where most of the kids in 7H had never been, or at least not by themselves. If you get out of the neighborhood, she'd tell them, they don't bother you about any curfew!

This reportage both pleased and shocked 7H, who somehow began to think that if old Melanie could roam around downtown and talk about her aunt, maybe they could too; if not right now, then someday—it wasn't unthinkable any more.

She always ended her stories in the bus station. There she would always think, she told her listeners, whether or not she shouldn't just get on one of them buses and go somewheres. Where? What to do? Just wherever that bus is going, Melanie would tell them, it don't matter to me. Even Roy would shut up then; it was too damn exciting to laugh about.

But as I say, after those two weeks she just wasn't around any more. We weren't usually informed about what happened to kids who dropped out, but of course 7H had their own idea.

(33) Time's Winged Chariot, with Plantation Club

February and March are dull times in the morning sports page—nothing but the interminable scoring of pro basketball teams and a vague sense of something about minor-league hockey. The season made itself felt at GW at least superficially. It was the beginning of the second semester and although it was impossible to see just how, it was clear that except for the nonregular wing of 9D we were pretty stable. It wasn't a big change.

7H still made as much noise coming up the stairs, they still panicked about the roll slips, still defended against surprise attacks about reading, still lugged the World Book down in volumes from the library shelves; in 9D May and the regulars still worked steadily toward the promised land though, and 7H now demanded their schedule even if, on schedule, they refused to do what they were spozed to. They wanted to know what they were rejecting. Only the radicals, led or perhaps only symbolized by Verna, still toyed with cosmetics, criticism and the number of angels who could dance on the head of a pin.

It looked like a stalemate. Yet any kind of theory of history would have told us differently, and even the sports page began to tell us that some baseball team was contemplating a trade, a new manager; indeed, we had a few changes too about this time.

With the second semester, for instance, we finished with Social Studies in 7B and began a semester of science. Opal Jameson now came into her glory as caretaker of our equipment for the miraculous experiments and demonstrations which I painstakingly figured out in theory from the manuals and which Opal herself actually made work. Under her capable hands and air of exasperation the coil and nail magnets worked like they spozed to, the balloons inflated and deflated over the fire, the gas bubbling in the pan actually turned out to be oxygen or hydrogen or carbon dioxide, the wood splinters flamed or went out, the gallon cans crushed themselves inward. I hadn't heard from Mrs. X or Mrs. Y; nothing had been forthcoming from Grissum about the voice lessons; no one had visited my room. Skates's attitude toward GW had soured a bit. He began writing applications to other districts, claiming that inevitable (and therefore right) as the existence of The Tribe was "under capitalism," that didn't make them any easier to be around.

In 8B Ruth began to be impossible about every third day. She'd gotten along quite well all year, causing, it's true, minor disturbances almost every period, but she'd always been willing to stop, satisfied, apparently, with little demonstrations of power. Stopping was what counted. She had even been a rather good student, in terms of 8B—she liked recitation, "giving answers," and was always willing to talk about stories we read in class, mainly, it's true, in order to point out how stupid one of the characters had been. These days she seemed determined to carry on every argument all period; that was going to be all we could talk about, who did what and to whom, whose fault everything was, why she didn't have to give back the other kid's shoes or jacket or pencil. Since the rest of 8B used her as an excuse to raise hell, I couldn't allow her this luxury and sent her out of the room or to the office. I had to stop that, though, because she made a terrible racket in the hall, or came back from the office with long tales about what she told Miss Bentley and what Miss Bentley said about you, Mr. Herndon. . . .

Finally I began sending her over to Skates's room once in awhile. Skates rather enjoyed arguing with her and she liked him; he flattered her and almost always put her in a good humor so that she could come back in ten or fifteen minutes happy as hell, telling me briefly how smart Skates had said she was and what a lousy teacher I was in contrast to Mr. Skates. Thus we held the line with her into March, but in the second week of March she indulged herself in the Plop Reflex twice.

In 9D Leon LaTore stopped coming to class—not just to my period. He didn't come to any classes. He didn't stop coming to school. He came on time, and spent the day roaming the halls or the yard, joining his class at passing periods to talk, going with them, stopping short at the door of whatever classroom they went into, and going on. He had been gloomy, sarcastic and disapproving all year, sitting in the back saying Sh! at all proposals, otherwise disturbing no one, simply uncommunicative and withdrawn. He now became the brand-new subject for the intellectuals of 9D, for the odd thing was that Leon Latore didn't come to class the rest of the year. Everyone knew that the teachers sent in slips on him, but nothing happened. He didn't stop coming to school, he didn't go to the office or to the counselors, or if he did (the kids swore he didn't) nothing resulted from it, he didn't go to Juvi—he didn't go anywhere, just kept on wandering the halls and the yards, eating lunch in the cafeteria like everyone else. Kids began to speak of students beaten up by him, of teachers threatened in the halls, of his talk about setting the fires in the big cans in the halls, which now became almost daily events, but nothing happened. In the teachers' room it was spoken of as a scandal. Something had better be done, was the consensus, before all the kids quit coming to class. In that opinion—that something should be done—they were in agreement with the nonregulars of 9D, who said that Leon LaTore was going to get into trouble if he didn't watch out.

Skates told me that a number of his ninth-graders were coming in after lunch half drunk, and the kids all said they were buying wine from Leon LaTore at a nickel a drink. Skates was in favor of the whole thing, both because it was a revolutionary act and because the student drunks were too sleepy in class to cause any trouble or make any noise.

I agreed with Skates that just being around The Tribe was an exhausting task, and perhaps Leon LaTore agreed too and decided he too had had enough of it; after all he wasn't getting paid.

I began to stop regularly at the Plantation Club after school for a beer or two. I wasn't riding with Skates for the time being—he'd moved out on his old landlady and was unsettled; he couldn't be responsible for getting anywhere on time right then.

The Plantation had South Seas decor, a good jukebox and was dark and warm. There were always several businessmen from the Negro hotel next door—a traveling man's hotel, as the bartender said. The men talked about their prospects, about what was happening in town, in other towns. The bartender often treated me in an extravagant Uncle Tom manner; at these times he would hurry to serve me, wipe off the bar over and over, ask me if the beer was cold enough, if I was comfortable, if the music was too loud or not loud enough. At other times he would ignore me completely when I came in, waiting until the last minute before I would begin to think about getting up to leave, at which instant he would hurry over and become Uncle Tom again. I couldn't see any resemblance between the salesmen here and The Tribe, and indeed whenever I tried to imagine The Tribe grown up I found I couldn't do it. I could only imagine them now; Skates would have said I had no sense of history. I counted on something happening in my classes and soon, hoping I could hold out long enough for it. I counted on it. It did occur to me now that perhaps it wouldn't; there were too many things against it, the school structure, other teachers, America itself. Even if it happened, I couldn't imagine the eventual result, if any. What difference would it make, would my teaching make, in their grown-up lives? I didn't care. I wouldn't have been able to say if I wanted them to turn into the salesmen at the Plantation or not.

Well, I waited to see what would happen with Leon LaTore. His actions weren't exactly in line with Grissum's ideas of order, certainly—it was an interesting confrontation, the more so since all I had to do was to keep on sending in the absence slips.

Life was getting more difficult at GW. The halls were noisier, there were more fights and more fires, classrooms were harder for teachers to control. The talk in the teachers' room was entirely about unruly students. Assemblies were canceled for all time, announced Grissum from the stage in the middle of the last one, evoking a chorus of Sh!

7H became personally involved in things when two bottles of wine were found in Roy's locker after some drunken culprit informed on him, and Roy went off for two weeks. According to 7H, who told the story in their usual mixture of glee, envy and regret, the counselors had to chase Roy twice around the field before they finally caught up with him. According to Alexandra, who admired Roy because she couldn't whip him, Roy was selling the wine for Leon LaTore. The wine itself was one of those new brands of sweet-tasting, cheap, high-alcohol-content stuff put out and advertised by large California wineries with a direct appeal to Negroes; I told Skates that at a nickel a drink they couldn't make any money from the sales, but he said that the point of capitalism wasn't to make money any more but merely to keep business going, and that Leon LaTore was simply doing what any intelligent man could see was the trend.

Along with all this, however, the spring was to bring us some happenings in 9D and an addition to 7H. These turned out to be what I'd been looking for all along, and are entitled Slambooks, Top Forty, Cinderella and Movie Day in the following chapters.

(34) Slambooks

I still have an ordinary yellow-covered notebook which used to belong to Cerise. Open the cover, and there is a page decorated in ink with curlicues and flourishes which inclose a paragraph. The paragraph states that "This is the Slambook belonging to Cerise, who says that nobody can read it without her permission and also anyone who steals it is guilty of a crime." It was all spelled correctly and signed in an elegant and unreadable script.

On the next page there is a list, numbered, of the students of 9D, and this is the key to what follows. For on each of the following pages there is the name of a kid, and on that page other kids have been invited to comment on his or her character, appearance, courage, brains or wealth, signing themselves only with a number corresponding to the key in the front. The beauty of this system is that the owner of the Slambook may then show the comments to the kid whose name is at the top of the page and have the pleasure of listening to him beg and plead with her to see the first page so that he may identify the commentators, the girl who said he was good-looking or the boy who said he was chicken. The authors of the remarks can also plead for her not to show that first page, and the owner thus becomes the center of frantic social activity.

I picked this Slambook up from the floor after the class left one period; when I gave it back to Cerise the next day, saying I didn't want to be guilty of a crime, she said it was already out of date and she had another, so I could have it.

Slambooks suddenly took precedence over everything. The Three C's had them one day; everyone else was making them the next. Since this was more work than many had done the entire year, I was delighted. They were avidly writing in them, not perhaps in complete sentences or according to the other standards expected for classwork, but the books were carefully made, the names spelled right, the style of the opening paragraph elegant and complicated and formal. The socializing surrounding them was also somewhat more restrained than usual, for the Slambooks had to be read, not just talked about, and also because shouting and threatening didn't do any good since the owner could then pretend to be insulted and refuse to disclose the contents or the key. All of the regulars fled the window area with its complete sentences and syllables and made their own Slambooks, so the activity was general. From the appearance and behavior of the class they might have been involved in some kind of engrossing class project or group work, discussing their progress with each other, and writing entries into notebooks to be reported on later with the results of their research, discussion and inquiry.

I wasn't invited to see the contents, of course, but I had Cerise's book and read it thoroughly, turning back to the front to identify the authors. I had to admit it was a pretty interesting way to spend a class period. I had expected to see a series of fairly nasty remarks, plenty of sexual invitation, and much bad talk in general; the expectation was based on the general prejudice we bring to anything teen-agers do of their own accord, and to the particular teen-agers of GW especially, and so it was wrong. I was shown again, for perhaps the hundredth time, that 9D was a group of children, not of dangerous hoodlums. In Cerise's book, only middle-aged May and revolutionary Leon LaTore compelled real improprieties. Someone had written "big tit" on May's page, and Verna had written a contemptuous "fuck him" on Leon LaTore's. Insult was taken care of in the traditional way with "big lip" and "monkey" getting their share of space. Still, even insults were usually compensated for; Robert, for instance, in addition to being called "the little black boy" and "too white," drew the admiring comment from Verna "Don't mess with him if you want to live." Several kids drew remarks like "smart cookie" and "plenty brains," or the reverse—"Think he smart, but I know better," or "Too dumb." It was always news to me in 9D if someone was thought unusually intelligent or the reverse. However, the bulk of the comment and most of the admiring remarks concerned the areas of looks and clothes. The three C's were tops, naturally: "Boss hair," "boss lips," "boss clothes," "boss complexion" appeared over and over again on their pages, the word "boss" having replaced "tough" sometime during the year as the hip synonym for good, beautiful, etc. The rest of the girls drew quite a bit of unfavorable comment about hair or head, but something good was always found by someone —they were discovered to have boss legs or boss clothes or something.

The boys were generally judged on the score of their manliness, athletic ability or personality and the word to describe their good qualities was usually the word "bad." Bad, in the Slambooks, meant either actually tough ("Think he bad!") or something like grown-up or mature ("He handsome and bad!") or that he was very good at something ("Bad man with a basketball!")

It's probably useful to comment on another aspect of the Slambooks—that is, they were a good demonstration of my relations with the other teachers at GW. We'd gone through, or would go through, the yo-yo season, the water-gun season, the paper-plane season, the clothespin-gun season and had duly confiscated all of these articles and tried in our various ways to stamp out these unruly activities. The whole talk now in the teachers' room was about Slambook season and voices rose in excited competition about how many had been confiscated or destroyed and how many wastebaskets and drawers they'd filled with Slambooks, and also how wasteful of time and materials Slambooks were and how difficult they made instruction. Methods for ridding GW of Slambooks forever were discussed and, I guess, tried out.

The trouble was that at the same time these discussions were going on full blast down in the teachers' room, I was likely to be up with 9D being delighted that they were finally writing something down, pleased with the general and rather orderly activity in the room and interested in the results, which seemed to me at least as accurate as, say, a sociogram. Anyway, this made serious discussion with those teachers rather difficult, not to say irrelevant; they were trying to put a stop to the very activity I was encouraging. It didn't bother me or make me angry—they weren't trying to stop it in my room, having all they could do to handle their own aspiring writers, and their attitude was consistent with what they'd always said they believed, thought, about their own classes.

Again, I'd been in there with 9D too long; all I could see was that they'd finally come across something that needed to be written down to be successful or interesting to them, which couldn't even exist without writing, and they were doing it as enthusiastically as possible.

(35) Top Forty

The reason for the Slambooks' existence was that it was Slambook season. It had nothing to do with me—I only welcomed it.
It was the same with the next event in 9D, which began around
the same time. It was, I think, the day I started reading Cerise's
book that Estelle came in the room and, instead of going over to
sit down, went to the board and began to write a list of current
popular songs on it.

Estelle was a tall, big girl, middle in the hierarchy of skin
color, hair, features, etc., and middle in other ways too. She
wasn't a regular, being too hip for that, but neither was she an
out-and-out radical. Not being one of the Three C's, who were
just themselves and felt they needed no other identity, she
belonged to the considerable portion of the class who might be
found one day with the regulars, another day grouped around
Verna, more often neither writing nor discussing great issues,
only sitting there in the class. This morning, as far as I could
tell, she simply felt like writing the tune titles on the board and
did it, in contrast to fifty other mornings she might have felt like
doing it and didn't.

The Top Forty, of course, were those forty rock-'n'-roll songs
played—over and over, all day long—by the disc jockeys of the
local rock-'n'-roll station. Estelle only planned to write down

the first twenty—at least that's all she did write down, and later on twenty became established as the proper number although we all still called it the Top Forty. It? Well, it soon became an it. As kids noticed Estelle chalking up titles, they began to question the validity of the action—as in, Mr. Herndon you going to let her do that?—and next to question her performance. They were sharp by now; all I had to do in answer to the first question was indicate their own activities with the Slambooks. There was immediate attention to proper spelling, proper order, simple correctness of Estelle's titles, and Estelle made a couple of changes. During this time, the first ten or fifteen minutes of the period, the class was going about its business with Slambooks, but Estelle had added a dimension. Top Forty became a thing, a program, like the pledge of allegiance (or a paragraph on the board for everyone to copy). Something everyone could expect to start the class with from now on, except of course that almost everyone thought it was something important in itself, which made the difference.

The next day there was an uproar due to the fact that some ten kids came dashing into class determined to put the Top Forty on the board. They shoved and argued and scrambled for space and chalk; four or five winners had already begun lists. Somehow it had been accepted that we were going to have Top Forty, but nothing had been done about who was going to do it. Estelle loudly claimed prior privilege; everyone knew she was right, but no one gave in. I had to order them all to their seats, shouting and yelling as Grissum correctly said. I said that if they wanted the list on the board, they'd have to figure out some way to do it without so much fuss. We didn't need more arguing and more noise, I submitted.

They began to argue about how to stop arguing. I kept out of it. Sometime during the debate Verna, who wasn't participating in it, came up to me asking something like what did I know about the Top Forty? Well, I knew quite a bit about it, since I listened to this same Top Forty every day on the way to school, and said so. She looked at me in her own way—which was a look that somehow said, I don't believe anything you say in advance, but I'll take a chance and ask anyway—and asked me if I liked rock 'n' roll. I told her I thought most of the songs were lousy, but that there were always one or two I really liked and that was more than I could say for any of the other popular music being written right then. So she asked, still suspending judgment, which ones of the current list, the one still not up on the board, I liked. I told her "Stagolee" particularly, and then too one by the Everly Brothers—I now forget what it was. She just nodded. It was one of the few times I'd spoken to her that she didn't say Sh! Encouraged, I went on to say that "Stagolee" came from an old song that had the words a little different and the tune a little different, but was about the same, and it was originally supposed to be about a real man.

Sh! said Verna scornfully, ending it. She knew that every song in the Top Forty was the newest thing there was, and all that about its being an old song was crap. I said, well, I had an old book at home that was full of old songs and it had this song "Stagolee" in it, so what about that? I have to see it before I believe it, she said. Bring it on down here.

I had the book all right, although it wasn't actually a very old book. It looked like the oldest book in the world though; a friend of mine once wrote down all the country and Western, cowboy, folk, hillbilly and blues tunes he knew, which was plenty, printed it in pencil or ink and bound it and sent it to me in Europe so I wouldn't forget all the songs we both knew. "Stagolee" was in there. Even if the book was only about five years old, that was older than the Top Forty by a long shot, and old enough for Verna.

When I brought it, the next day, she was impressed. That book so old they didn't even have no printing machines then, Mr. Herndon, she told me. She found "Stagolee," and asked me if she could keep the book for the day and I said OK. All through the period I could see her looking through the book at the songs, "The Great Speckled Bird," "The Wabash Cannonball," "Frog Went a-Courting" . . . I didn't feel bad about it; after all, "Stagolee" *was* a pretty old song.

After school she brought the book back. She told me she

guessed it was all right to use them old songs if they was good to start with, and if they brought them up to date. She'd checked to see if there were any more Top Forty songs in there but hadn't found any, although later on there were a few, "Irene" and "Frog Went a-Courting" I remember particularly. She asked me if I wanted those Top Forty tunes on the board every day. I said it was fine with me, but without all the uproar. She agreed with that. That all we do in this class is fuss, she said. Why do you let them fuss so? I said I thought if they could ever get it all out of their systems, they might stop. Otherwise, I said, they'd never really stop it; they'd just be waiting until I let go a second and there they'd be at it again. What was the good of that? I wanted to know.

Verna didn't agree. She didn't think they'd ever get it out of their systems one way or the other. However, if I wanted the Top Forty on the board, she would see they did it right and without no fussing.

We let it go at that. I remembered that in Cerise's Slambook, along with the remarks "big leg" and "tall and tough," someone had written under Verna's name *"The* Boss!"

(36) "Cinderella"

During library periods with my classes I kept looking in the
back storeroom for anything I could use with my classes. I
came across an entire series of playbooks containing familiar
stories dramatized; there were three volumes to the set, and
enough copies of each so that each kid in the class could have
one to use. We had used these off and on in 7B and 8B as a
kind of break, something different—reading them aloud, taking
the parts and often recording the performance and playing it
back for our amusement. I kept the whole set stacked in a
corner of the room, since the librarian said that no one else ever
used them, and occasionally kids from 9D or 7H would take a
look at them.

One of these days, near the beginning of the period in 9D,
with the regulars hard at work or not-work, the Slambooks
going through their courses, the Top Forty being laboriously
written on the board under the watchful eye of Verna and a few
critics, I was astonished to see the Three C's approaching my
desk in a body. It was, to my knowledge, the first time during
the year they had voluntarily left their table at all, let alone
come near the teacher's desk. They were all three clutching
playbooks and asked me why couldn't we read these plays out
loud in class, everyone taking the parts?

Why not? I'd already tried to get 9D interested in play-reading some time before, but the radicals weren't interested and the regulars hadn't the time to spare. So I said it was a fine idea, but who was going to do the reading?

It was an idiotic question. With the Three C's planning to do something, everyone in the class was suddenly eager to take part. The C's own big table was quickly moved up to the front of the room—ten boys shoving each other for the honor of grabbing hold of it—desks shoved out of the way, folding chairs set around it. Trouble began as twenty kids dived for space around the table. I yelled. Everyone finally fell back, and taking the easy way out, I announced that the Three C's, having introduced the idea, could pick out the players. There followed plenty of threats and counterthreats, some refusals-in-advance-of-expected-rejection, an incipient Plop Reflex or two; the C's finally extorted enough promises from about ten individuals, and, with perhaps fifteen minutes left in the period, they began to read the play. That was the first time I realized that the play the C's were so excited about was "Cinderella."

It was a terrible reading all the way around. Unprepared, the kids stumbled and read too fast, giggled among themselves or argued, forgot their turns in haste to correct someone else, and the audience, prepared at first to listen, soon lost interest and drifted back to their spellers, Slambooks and cosmetics.

The source of the trouble was the Three C's, naturally. In their haste they had picked "Cinderella" because they saw there was a Prince and a fancy-dress ball and two sisters who were going to that ball; they saw themselves starring—dancing, dining, diamonds shining and all. They weren't prepared to find Cinderella the heroine and had given that part to a girl named Grace, not concealing the fact that Grace looked, in their opinion, like someone who stayed home and cleaned up all the time. As the play went on and Grace steadily read all the most interesting parts with the Fairy Godmother and the Prince, the C's became more and more upset and began to interpose remarks. How could the Prince dance with that ugly old thing? they wanted to know.

By the end of the play they had really become the jealous sisters, so much so that they were almost speechless when the Prince began to go around with the glass slipper, trying it on all the ladies in the town. Unlike the sisters in the play, the Three C's knew it was going to fit on that ugly old Grace's foot—they could see how this was going to end.

When the Prince got to their house and tried the slipper on the first of the mean sisters, he was supposed to read the line, "Oh no! Your foot is much too big for this slipper. You cannot be the lady I seek!" This came as a surprise to the first sister, Charlene, who was too irritated now to pay attention to the text, but by the time the Prince got as far as "big" Charlene jumped up in a fury and yelled, Don't you say my feets too big, you black monkey! and slammed her book down.

That broke up the play. Everyone began to laugh and yell Whooo-eee! The other two C's, having looked ahead now and seen the same fate reserved for them, quit the play too. We ain't playing no part where they get to say our feet too big, Mr. Herndon! The bell rang about then, and the class rushed out still yelling Whooo-eee!, planning to tell everyone about the play and about the C's big feet. They left "Cinderella" scattered about the room, the chairs knocked over, the table still up in front.

I left the table there. The next day the C's tried to recruit someone to move it back for them, but the class objected. A number of them had playbooks out and were planning to read another play. But first, they called out to me, we got to finish that one about Cinderella. They wanted to know how it came out.

(37) Movie Day

With the advent of science in 7B I began to show them a lot of films. I felt I didn't know very much about quite a few areas of science and ought to try everything; also many of the science films were a pleasure to watch. Ever since Brotherhood Week 7H had been clamoring for films, and I occasionally showed one—a storytelling film, some legends and myths, puppet plays. I was stuck on the idea of getting films which had some relevance to English as if we were a real English class, and there weren't many interesting ones. 7H straightened me out as soon as they saw the stacks of film cans which appeared in the room. They wanted to see them all. Those are science films, I told them. Didn't they see those films in science?

7H didn't listen to that kind of talk. Here they were, and there were the films. Let's get started seeing 'em.

We got started. We began to see all kinds of films—at first, of course, all them science movies. They were by far the best of the school films, being often quite new and usually in color. We saw them films about rubber plantations, about farm machinery, floods, rockets, geology, animals—everything. 7H was especially pleased with the animal and seashore films, which were universally thought beautiful. One film in particular—from Bell Telephone, about weather—was a great favorite. In it an old professor was explaining winds and fog and all to some children, and he was constantly interrupted by indignant animated figures representing North Wind, South Wind, a goddess, the Old Man of the Sea and so on, who insisted that it was they, not the professor's hot and cold air masses, who were responsible for which way the wind blew. 7H was almost charming, discussing the film on the basis of who was right in the argument, and we showed it lots of times.

Certain subjects were less popular. Films showing blood or one-celled animals or bacteria under a microscope both frightened and disgusted 7H. One particular film which showed cells surrounding and devouring alien organisms made several of them ill and the rest considered it too scary. On the other hand, the habits of bears and "The Red-Winged Blackbird" made everyone happy and made up for the occasional discomforts of science.

Somehow Friday got established as Movie Day; the films were usually short, and we could often show three in a period. Like the events of 9D I'm not sure how it happened. It must have come about quite gradually, but it seems to me that all of a sudden we were having Movie Day and that this Movie Day had certain characteristics, none of them determined or agreed upon by me. 7H was still sticking to the schedule, of course: reading or language groups, library, recording (to which they began to add the playbooks)—reading-group day might be a day of complete uproar when no group could do any reading at all, but it was still reading-group *day*—but their idea was the more schedule the better, and Movie Day was easily added into the scheme.

It turned out that the scheduled and approved activity during Movie Day was, besides the film itself, eating. I remember Alexandra stating happily to me one day, Mr. Herndon, on Movie Day we get to bring our candy and our gum and corn chips and eat 'em while the movie going on. Since we'd always had a problem in 7H about eating in class, I couldn't quite see where she got that idea. However, the class was 100 percent agreed; it had already been decided.

Who made that decision? How? I've no idea. All of a sudden there was 7H sitting nicely in the back of the room watching the screen, desks pulled up in front of them on which were piled bags of chips, sacks of candy and so on.

It was a party. Obviously they had figured out beforehand who was going to bring what. They didn't want to have all corn chips, say, and no M & M's. Someone had to bring the drinks. Not everyone could bring something that time, some being temporarily out of funds, so everything was being shared. You can't have a party if some people are left out—it wasn't to be like just everyone that could afford it chewing on something in class.

There they sat in the dark, watching the Four Winds arguing with the professor. I could hear them passing around the sacks, crunching up the chips, opening up the cans of root beer and orange. A pleasant and quiet social chatter arose from them as they commented on the film, the quality of the food, how everyone looked in the dark. It was miraculous. It was also completely illegal.

I should have put a stop to it immediately, of course. On the other hand, I didn't really have a chance to. There hadn't been any official decisions about it beforehand where I could get in there and forbid something—no committees or class meetings or democratic decisions or any of the other usual means teachers employ to get the kids to agree to what the teacher wants and the school condones. In order to forbid it I would have had to forbid this accomplished fact—turn off the projector, turn on the lights, collect the edibles, move the desks back and ruin everything.

I wasn't up to it. For, of course, included in that everything I would be ruining would have to be not only the pleasant but illegal party, but also the very thing I'd thought hopelessly about back at the post office and at the Plantation Club and even at home: I would have to ruin and forbid the solidarity of 7H which all of a sudden existed right before my eyes on Movie Day.

(38) May Day!

Springtime at GW was the time for riots. The Tribe had given up and was becoming violent. By April the story of the year was over—some details, some dramatics left to tell, but the score was already in. All the promises had lost their appeal and The Tribe was busting out. Fights. Fires. Broken windows. Food thrown all over. Neighborhood complaints about vandalism. Teachers who had kept things in check all year began to have their troubles. We began to hear about So-and-so who was threatened by a group of kids, someone else who was swung on by a student, another who hit some kid. Down the hall old Mrs. Z was knocked flat in the hall by a girl whom she'd ordered down to the office for chewing gum. She'd ordered that girl and all the rest of them down to the office all year long, but now she had ordered once too often. Riots began to take place in the rooms—books torn up and papers thrown around, desks overturned and pushed out into the halls, the helpless teacher calling for assistance. Oddly enough, the faculty took it in stride. It happens every year, they seemed to say. We try. We hold 'em for as long as we can. . . .

Skates was an exception to the general fatalistic mood. The paragraph to copy didn't do the trick these days, the kids weren't going along with jokes and bantering. One day during a hard spring rain his afternoon class began to raise hell. They did the usual—tore up books, scattered the contents of cabinets all over, threw paper out the window. Skates gave up and dashed out of the room to get help, and the kids locked him out. By the time he got back in with the aid of the custodian and Mr. Grisson, the contents of his desk had been thrown out the window too, the desk itself overturned, his grade book torn up, and so on. Jim, he told me, it was a real, honest-to-God riot.

Skates's feelings were really hurt. Why me? he asked me over and over again. Why me?

I'm on their side, he kept saying. He was really upset. One detail of the riot, which he took to be directed at him personally, bothered him more than the rest. The kids had thrown his hat out the window along with the rest of the stuff; it had sailed down into the gutter. When Skates got back in the room and looked out the window, there he saw his hat floating in that muddy water along with the papers and books, and somehow it was that sight which was too much for him. He was almost crying as he told me about it. They threw my hat out! he kept saying. Why did they want to throw out my hat?

He'd always felt that he and The Tribe were just passing the time together while waiting for history to catch up with them; the idea was to make the time pass pleasantly and offer mutual support in the meantime. If there were irritating or troublesome moments along the way, that was OK with him, for basically he liked the kids just as they were, just as he really liked the idea of jitney girls. The majority of the teachers were different, of course, and they weren't affected personally at all. They had believed all along that there was a war going on; outnumbered, they used every trick and all the moral authority granted them by the school and the country of America to hold the fort as long as it might be held. Now, retreating, still punishing the enemy whenever possible, giving ground, they hadn't given up and they weren't depressed. They would regroup, they told themselves, and come back next year for those battles, which they expected would follow the same pattern of war.

I viewed the daily slaughter with detachment and no little vanity. If at the end of the story the other teachers were beginning to lose, I was just starting to win. If their programs were falling apart, we were just starting to move. I felt we'd been lucky again. The potential rioters in 7H and 9D didn't have time to riot now. They could have rioted with ease back in October or even February, but that hadn't been the rioting season. Now it was too late.

7H had their schedule to adhere to, and Movie Day activities to plan. If they did these things with a good deal of noise and what adults would have to call disorder, there was no more of either than before. In fact there was a good deal less; in order to plan for Movie Day, for instance, each kid had to give up a little on his right to panic and make a fuss. Movie Day was worth it. The point is that once we were inside the room, the general atmosphere of riot didn't affect us; by now I didn't give a damn what happened outside the classroom.

9D was busy every day with the playbooks. They not only read almost every day, but they were discussing—all right, they were arguing, squabbling, making a lot of noise, using a lot of bad language, not exactly abiding by *Robert's Rules of Order*—certain questions about play-reading. They were discussing who read well and why, they were telling each other what the play was about, they argued about where certain characters should sit at the table. The most important question to them was what relationship the reader should have to the character he was reading. Two solid factions arose; the first arguing that if the character was a giant, a big kid had to read the part. The second disagreed; they thought that if the character was a beautiful girl, any girl who *read* beautifully, who *sounded* beautiful, should read it. Mr. Herndon, someone would cry, Cerise want to sit in the middle because she the Queen, but Amy spozed to sit in the middle because she say the most! They came in the room, slammed down books and stood together in groups around the room telling each other things like It don't mean you have to have big feet just because you read the sister who got big feet, or You read like a monkey, you can *be* the monkey!

Their values had changed, as they say at State, like your values spozed to change whenever you have something you want to do. The Three C's, for instance, were hopeless when it came to getting the play done right. They always made the same mistake—choosing to be the Queen instead of the milkmaid, and then being disappointed and jealous when the Queen turned out to be mean and stupid and the milkmaid was the heroine. They could never choose to be the milkmaid and as a result were continually being insulted. The kids tried to keep them in the play without giving them enough to do to wreck things. The C's status outside the business of play-reading didn't change though. They were still the whitest, still had boss hair, boss lips and all that. 9D's values were completely realistic; unlike the Three C's, the rest of the class knew the difference between the play and the world.

The Slambooks had gone out of style by April. The Top Forty was proceeding as a matter of course, Verna's organization, whatever it had been, proving to be permanent.

Verna had taken over the management of play production. She didn't read herself nor did she really remain a part of the audience. During the reading she stood aside (in the wings, if we'd had wings), tall, frowning, critical, aloof, attentive, and after each reading she managed to get around to everyone and tell them what they'd done wrong. Compliments were not her style; a kid knew he'd read well, in Verna's opinion, if he was up there again the next time. Occasionally, it's true, she'd make a few general remarks addressed to no one in particular about how the play was good and that So-and-so was a good reader. Her system wasn't apparent—its details were not, anyway—but its purpose was to get plays read aloud in the class, kids reading them, certain kids doing it, without all that fussing. It wasn't particularly fair; certain kids read more than others, certain others who didn't want to read at all found themselves doing so because you spozed to read once in a while, not just sit on your fat ass and listen all the time. Her purpose was to produce a good reading of as many plays as possible, taking into account certain factors—people couldn't be allowed to get too mad and ruin everything, even bad readers had to be given a turn at least sometime, the powerful C's had to be accounted for, etc.

We were making it. Rolling. They weren't doing things the way a group of thirty-year-old teachers would do them, of course. They didn't even do them the way everyone seemed to think that kids should do them, with many a meeting, committee, schedule, discussion, and vote. Even looking back at these pages, I don't really know what brought them to it, but they were doing it, making their revolution in the class. I was enthusiastic, pleased, proud of them.

In this mood I met with Mr. Grisson in May for his official evaluation of my year's work. He opened the interview by stating that it was always painful to him to have to make judgments, but that evaluation was his job. It was best to be frank. In short he found my work unsatisfactory on every count; he could not recommend me for rehire in the district. Furthermore he must say that he considered me unfit for the position of junior high school teacher in any school, anywhere, now or in the future, and would so state on my evaluation paper.

(39) Order

The teacher's evaluation form has a number of statements on one side of it, each followed by two or three boxes to the right of it where a check mark can be placed. The boxes are labeled Satisfactory or Unsatisfactory, with sometimes an Excellent thrown in. I don't remember a lot about the form used (at GW); the statements in the first group were of the type *Classroom Management, Efficient Use of Supplies and Material, Maintains Classroom Control* or *Efficient Use of Class Time.* Next came things like *Cooperates With the PTA, Maintains Friendly Relations with Staff*—and last personal attributes like *Neat, Well-Groomed, Friendly Relations with Pupils,* etc.

As Grissum pointed out, it was the first ones that counted. Presumably you could learn to be neater or dress more fashionably, learn to get along with the other teachers, to have friendly relations with kids and all that. The PTA hadn't existed since the second semester, when it had disbanded because the only parents who ever came were the six mothers of the six girls with boss skin, hair, lips and clothes in the A group of the ninth grade, who were also the officers of the school.

You could even learn, Grissum said sometime during the interview, to control your class and use your time efficiently. To that end, learning, he'd suggested voice lessons for me, sent

Mrs. X and Mrs. Y down, demonstrated for me himself. When it became clear that I didn't want to learn to do any of this, there had been nothing to do but give up on me. That was why the voice lessons hadn't come about.

To his credit, he granted me a long interview and listened to everything I had to say. It's tempting now to write down a long conversation which I suppose I must have had with him, what he said, what I said—but I'd have to make it up. I really don't remember much that we said. On the form, where it counted, I was totally unsatisfactory. He spoke to the point; the children were not in their seats on time, they did not begin lessons promptly, many of them sat around doing nothing, there was not an atmosphere conducive to study, no effort was made to inculcate good study habits, there was no evidence of thorough preparation of lessons or goals. I appeared to encourage activities that were opposed to the efforts of the faculty in general, I appeared eager to discuss with the students matters irrelevant or unfit for the classroom, I had no control over their actions, and I steadfastly rejected aid and advice from experienced people.

I had to talk about results. What about the riots? I wanted to know. What was the good of saving all those materials, using them efficiently all year long, if at the end of the year they were all thrown out the window anyway? What good was the order of these experienced teachers if it ended up in chaos? No one in my class had rioted, I pointed out; no one locked me out, or threw my hat out the window. None of this happened in my classes. So who had the better control? I argued.

He wasn't impressed. He knew there had been riots, he knew that I'd had none. It didn't matter—in fact, it proved his point, he said. It was another case where my description was accurate but my conclusion wrong. A riot meant that some order had been imposed, some control established, since it was against that control that the children were rebelling. It followed that as I was allowing them to do as they pleased it was unnecessary for them to riot.

It was right then that I really understood that I was being fired. It hadn't really occurred to me before. Grissum wanted me to understand that he knew I had worked hard, that I was serious about what I was doing, that my character, intelligence and "dedication" weren't in question. What was?

It seemed a matter of ideas of order. This is a problem school, I do remember his saying. His job, and the job of the teachers, was to make it into something that was no longer a problem school. He was certain that was possible. It is the belief in this goal that counts, he told me. He used the word *belief* many times. No one is perfect, so a teacher may lose control once, twice, a hundred times, but if he believes in that control himself, that order, he will eventually win through.

To what? I wanted to know. I told him that he hadn't seen my classes since his demonstration, and I thought he should come up and take a look. I summarized what progress I thought we'd made, omitting the illegal details of Movie Day and hoping he didn't come on Friday. He said he would come, but I shouldn't think that would have any effect on my evaluation. For, supposing the class had worked out their own system of doing things, I should realize that wasn't what he thought desirable. The opposite, in fact.

Thinking back about what I've written about Grissum, not only right here but earlier, I realize I've not been able to make him seem human at all. It was just as if one of us was of some other species, a Martian perhaps; I imagine he had the same problem thinking about me. We talked together, Earthman and Martian, agreeing on everything except what to do.

What to do—or what we did. That was the real point, I guess. Skates, for instance, was unpredictable, wrongheaded, narrow-minded, rude, perhaps selfish, certainly one-way about nearly everything, in attitude, but essentially everything he did seemed to me human and sane. Grissum was personally quite affable, reasonable, courteous, tolerant and sensible—but his actions toward the school and The Tribe never really seemed to me to be human, nor, in the end, quite sane.

(40) "Cinderella" Again

9D blasted in as usual, carping and disorderly—all the old tricks still performed out of habit, a grab at a skirt, a snatch at a shoe, a taunt, an accusation. "Cinderella" was scheduled for performance for the third or fourth time.

Although we still had plays which hadn't been done, "Cinderella" was a favorite. They had a different attitude toward it now; it was like people who go to see *Don Giovanni* or an old movie—they knew how it came out by now, and could relax and enjoy the details.

Mr. Herndon! Maxine here! came a shout. Who was Maxine? I didn't know. Then I remembered her, a girl who'd been in the class for the first month perhaps and then dropped out, no one knowing why as usual. She stood around, not doing much. Regulars were getting out their books and paper; they were either planning to work, having had enough of "Cinderella," or else just making a show of it, planning to listen anyway. I went over to look at their work and assign something just in case. The class began to organize itself.

At the end of our interview Grisson had told me, just as we parted, that I seemed to have a good deal of rapport with the kids, and some real "insight" into their feelings or whatever. (He thought it might help me out quite a bit in some other type of work.) I was reminded of this statement when I looked up and watched 9D organizing itself.

It's really almost impossible for adults, and no doubt especially for adult teachers, to see anything "constructive" going on in a bunch of kids shouting at each other. All the adults can see is just that: kids, all bunched together, yelling at each other. You can't believe they are doing it for anything you'd call a purpose; they are simply creating a problem, something that shouldn't exist at all.

The adults also can't imagine that this problem is going to cease to exist unless they, the adults, make it cease. They feel that unless they issue orders and directions and threats, the kids will never stop making noise, never stop yelling, never get organized.

This feeling is wrong. The adults are wrong on both counts, not because they are stupid, not even because they lack what Grissum called "insight" either. They are wrong because almost no one can stand to wait around long enough without doing anything, so that they can see what all the shouting is about, or what might happen when it eventually is over. They can't stand to, and so they never find out. Never finding out, they assume that there was nothing there. I don't think the quality of insight is unique or even rare, Grissum to the contrary. What does seem to be rare is the ability to wait and see what is happening.

I admit 9D could probably outshout the rest of The Tribe, and The Tribe could outshout everyone else. There they were, about fifteen or so kids, all in a cluster, standing, shouting at each other, Verna in the middle shouting at all of them—a hundred demands, questions, orders, all at once. You couldn't make it out at all. Probably there were a hundred shouted irrelevancies, threats and insults too. But the fact is this outcry was orderly in intent and in effect, for in about four or five minutes it was all over, readers were sitting down, they had books, the audience was getting ready to listen. I doubt very much if 9D could have been organized to read a play in five minutes, even by an experienced teacher with a machine gun.

Just before they began, Maxine came up to me and asked if

she could sit at my desk, and since I usually sat at the back of the room during the readings, I said OK. I don't know why she wanted to sit there; you don't have to know everything.

The reading was about halfway through the play—after Cinderella had been to the ball and gotten back safely by midnight—at a point where the audience knows something that the mean sisters don't, which was an aspect of "Cinderella" that 9D liked a lot. All of a sudden the door opened with a bang and there stood Grissum, looking in as he had said he would. He stood there in the door, erect, unsmiling, while the readers faltered and stopped. He took a quick look around the room and then, when everything was silent, glared straight into the room. Glared; there was no question that he didn't like very much what he saw. We all knew it; we suddenly all felt pretty guilty. We wished we had been sitting up straight in our desks, all in rows, silent, diagramming sentences or writing out our spelling words. After perhaps twenty seconds he stepped back, closed the door, and was gone without saying a word.

Hell broke loose as it had once before in similar circumstances. It looked like I might get my riot after all. The readers rose up, playbooks were slammed down, kids started for each other, a desk fell. Robert ran across in front of me, chasing someone; I was as mad as the rest of them, so I grabbed him by the jacket. It was a mistake. Let go my goddam jacket! he yelled, struggling to get free. I got a better grip and yelled: Shut up, Robert! Now sit down! Let go my jacket, he screamed, and gave a great wrench, at which the jacket tore with a loud rip. Robert looked down at his jacket and, in the sudden silence as everyone saw what was going on, he shouted: You tore my jacket, you black motherfucker!

So no riot today; that stopped everything. Oooooh? from all sides. Robert stood there. But it was all too much for me, and I began to laugh. It summed up the entire year with The Tribe— the first days, through the library, and the riots and Grisson's ideas of order up to Robert's summation, the last resort, the supreme comment and insult: not *motherfucker,* of course, but *black.*

I sat down at a desk; the class waited for catastrophe. I ignored them and they began, after a time, to relax. Later I could hear them, as so many times before, beginning to talk about what Robert had said, what I had said, how it started, whose fault it was, what they would have done, why I laughed —the last ten minutes of a late round with 9D, intellectual and disorderly at the bell.

Verna visited my room after the bell for lunch with an added touch to the day. She asked me if I'd heard about Maxine. When I said no, she told me that Maxine had just had a miscarriage—looking at me to let me know she knew the word—in old Mrs. Z's room down the hall.

(41) Nothing Personal

I spent an afternoon downtown with the district personnel officer, who convinced me to resign peacefully instead of making them go to the trouble of firing me. He deplored the fact of a "personality conflict" which had no doubt been the cause of my poor rating, but he didn't offer me a job with some other personality type in the district.

It wasn't until the next day at noon that I realized that the personnel man's advice wasn't so good either. He said that if I was fired it would look rather bad on my record and I might have more trouble getting another job than if I just resigned, which was, after all, my privilege. He was sympathetic, but in his sympathy forgot that alongside my resignation Grissum's statement that I was "unfit" to teach kids of junior high school age might look pretty bad; they might as well have ridden me out of town on a rail. But, as I say, we both forgot that detail and settled things amicably; I cursed myself for it that noon.

I spent the hour walking around the streets nearby; I'd suddenly had enough of GW Junior High. I began to imagine to myself what Grissum had seen when he looked in my room during "Cinderella"—when he looked at a scene which I was offering up as some great achievement! He saw some sixteen or seventeen kids slouched in desks here and there throughout the room wherever they felt like sitting. He saw one girl sitting at the teacher's desk and the teacher himself at the back of the room at a kid's desk. None of them, teacher included, were doing anything, except perhaps listening to about ten other kids hunched around a table reading a child's fairy tale in their various unimproved accents. No writing, no paragraphs, no workbooks, no recitation, no lessons, no rows, no teaching, no taking notes, no learning, no reading, at least not of anything that mattered—not a goddam thing except that goddam "Cinderella."

The more I thought about "Cinderella," the madder I got. Those playbooks were full of the kinds of stories and fairy tales every kid in America knows by heart by the time he's eight or ten at the most. "Rumpelstiltskin," "Snow White," "The Three Sillies," "The Little Mermaid," "Seven at One Blow," "Jack the Giant Killer," "Gawain and the Green Knight," "The Tin Soldier"—part of the cultural heritage, as they say. Everyone already knew them, and it was a waste of time for those ninth-graders to read that stuff.

The only trouble was that 9D didn't know them at all. Like 7H and "Cowboy Small," they somehow hadn't inherited these epics. 9D was mainly interested in these works because they wanted to know how they came out. What would the witch do? Would the Princess guess the dwarf's name? Snow White awaken? They read them aloud because they were plays and spozed to be read aloud; they liked them because they hadn't heard them before, and after they'd heard them they liked them because they were good.

So I was angry at Grisson for not seeing this and for breaking up our reading. I was mad at myself for being a fool and not realizing that I was going to have to satisfy someone besides 7H and 9D in this particular world. Most of all I was furious at The Tribe, for not being able to do anything the way you spozed to. Why couldn't they sit in rows and hear the play? Why hadn't they read "Cinderella" at age six or seven or eight and let me alone with it and the idiotic Top Forty, written and edited their compositions, answered questions and shut up? Why, with all this fuss about what they spozed to *get,* didn't they ever plan on doing what they spozed to *do* without a series of tantrums? Why couldn't they read? Why couldn't they admit it, that they couldn't? Why keep on with eye-watering and lipreading and making life miserable for everyone?

7H had to take it. I shouted them into their seats, cutting off their entering frolic. I lectured them about doing their part. I told them they required immense tolerance of me, but weren't willing to attempt anything of the slightest difficulty. I told them their misbehavior was only an alibi to avoid the simple responsibilities of every other school kid in the country.

It's surprising how easily this kind of talk comes, once you begin. They reacted correctly at first, hanging their heads, waiting silently for it to be over with and to get on with the period; after a little while, though, they had trouble keeping it up, not being used to it with me and not quite believing it either. One kid got up; Roy began to laugh. Come on, Mr. Hern-don, someone said, we ain't that bad.

Once started though, I couldn't get over it that easily, and when I heard someone begin to giggle over to my left I hauled off without looking and slammed whoever it was backhanded across the head. There was a yell from the kid; oooooh? went the class. I looked, and saw Vincent halfway out of his seat where I'd knocked him. He rushed out the door, crying and yelling he was going to tell the principal on me.

Everyone shouted at me at once, mostly to the effect that I shouldn't have slugged old Vincent of all kids, but Roy or Wade or Alexandra instead.

It was true, of course. I felt I didn't give a damn; it was I who was getting fired, not Vincent, not 7H. During all the advice and criticism Vincent marched back in, still sniveling but standing up straight, and stomped to his seat. He was a big hero. I felt like knocking him out of it again.

Instead I came off it. I made everybody shut up. I felt bad now about slugging Vincent, and told them so, but there wasn't anything I could do about it now. I told Vincent I was sorry, and that I didn't mean to hit him personally; that I just felt like hitting somebody and he was just in the right place at the wrong time. After some discussion, 7H seemed to accept that as reasonable.

(42) Ruth

It was only right that there should be a few dramatics left for the end of the year, and fitting, also, that Ruth should have a share in them. Rumors and warnings about Ruth had been a part of daily life at GW since Ruth's own warning to me before school even started. During the year I heard she had put a fifth-grade teacher in a mental hospital, caused a sub to leave the room screaming, knocked a kid's teeth out. I heard that she was really twenty-one, fourteen, and all ages in between, that she had dropped out of school for one year, three years, that she had had a baby, an abortion, an affair with a male teacher at GW, been a prostitute for students in a house across the street. None of these were Skates's inventions. He stuck to his own story about her.

One afternoon a crowd of yelling kids outside the school announced a fight in progress. It turned out that Ruth and another girl were fighting and that Ruth was beating the other girl badly. Grisson, the secretary and two other women teachers happened to be around—one of the teachers was the homemaking teacher (Negro) and the other actually the nurse (white)— and had gone out to break it up. When they got there the other girl was in bad shape and scared worse; it was decided that

Grisson would take her home and the rest would conduct Ruth into the office.

After about ten minutes in the office, the teacher and the nurse decided to leave Ruth with the secretary to await Grisson's return. They were going home.

(Here I have to say that I didn't see any of this myself; the reports are from the three people involved—secretary, nurse, and teacher.)

But when they made for the door, Ruth said, according to all three, You ain't going nowheres.

Now, Ruth, they all said.

If I got to stay, you got to stay, said Ruth.

Argument began, the women saying Now, Ruth, again and trying to make her see reason, Ruth simply repeating that if she stayed, they all stayed. They gave up and turned to go anyway, at which Ruth jumped up, grabbed an office chair, swung it over her head threateningly, and allowed as how they weren't going nowhere. They tried to talk, but Ruth was through with talk.

She ordered them all out of the office. If they didn't do what she said, she was going to bust them over the head with that chair. They went. She ordered them into a nearby open classroom and, inside, ordered them to sit down. She remained standing, the chair over her head, leaning it against the wall over her head. Those school-office chairs are heavy chairs. As they sat there, they said later, she lectured them a mile a minute about who was doing the ordering now, and told them what their heads would look like if and when that chair hit them. They were terrified, they admitted. They kept wondering when Grisson was coming back; what could be taking him so long? Ruth kept them there for—their reports vary—a half hour, twenty minutes, forty-five minutes.

Abruptly, Ruth let them go. She didn't say why. Now you can go, she said, putting the chair down, opening the door and going out herself. You going because I *let* you go, she said, turning around just once to tell them.

The three were heroes for a few days, and the faculty became intellectuals too and discussed what had happened, what should have happened, what they would have done. There was a brief undercurrent of suspicion: Where was Grisson all this time? Certainly he would have handled it . . .

Ruth herself was out of school for a week, but returned in time to be promoted with the rest of 8B to the ninth grade.

(43) Harvey

Let me say clearly in advance that I don't know how Harvey learned to read. I don't know when he learned. I couldn't say this method worked or that one, whether phonics or word recognition, reading groups, flash cards, tape recorder, structural linguistics, or "Cowboy Small."

On one of those last days, a commotion came from his reading group. I went over. Harvey stood up and announced to me, Mr. Hern-don, I can so read! Everyone jeered, with some justification. It wasn't as if Harvey had ever admitted he couldn't read.

You go on and test me, Mr. Hern-don! cried Harvey. That was new, so I went over and got a copy of *Red Feather*. I turned to a page I was pretty sure he hadn't memorized and gave it to him. He held it standing up and, sure enough, began to read it. It was a section where Red Feather, the Indian boy, is learning to make arrows from the old arrow maker. I could remember reading it myself as a child. Harvey read about making the shaft straight by pulling it through a hole bored in a block of hardwood or a piece of sandstone, I can't remember which. He stumbled a little, stopped and puzzled, moving his lips, but he read it. Everyone knew he was reading, not just reciting something he knew by heart.

When he finished I said, We ought to give Harvey a hand. Everybody clapped and cheered; naturally there were a few calls of *watermelon-head* and *chump* mixed in. After the ovation Harvey couldn't shut up; he was in a daze. He kept talking like a reformed drunkard, telling about how bad things were when he couldn't read, how he knew all the letters, but put them together and they just didn't mean anything to him *before,* but *now* . . . and what he planned to read next . . . them comics . . .

Finally someone couldn't stand it any more and yelled out, Harvey, why don't you shut up! You ain't nothing but a little colored boy!

That tore it! I thought. But Harvey didn't care. He had a big, pink ringworm spot on his forehead, I remember, and he said reasonably, just as if it weren't completely unheard of at GW, I know I'm just a little colored boy. What about it?

(44) A Few Last Words

On the last day of school, Hazel and Ramona told me I was the nicest and best teacher they ever had. I told them I bet they said that to all their teachers; the class agreed loudly that they did.

After lunch a couple of men met me at the door to my classroom and introduced themselves as officials from the union. They'd heard I was being fired and wanted to know if I wanted to fight it. I thought it was a little late for them to be coming around. They admitted that was true, but said they had a big case coming up for two or three Negro teachers who were in the same boat and they hadn't been able to get around to me. The idea was to fight the cases on the grounds of racial prejudice; I could see I wouldn't do them any good there. I told them it was pointless anyway, since there wasn't any use in my working with Grisson. I had other things to do, I told them. Keep up the good work for the union! they encouraged me, and we left it at that.

Later I heard they had lost the case, which was no surprise. There had been plenty of other Negro teachers rehired. I didn't think there was any significant prejudice against Negro teachers in the district; if the Negro teachers didn't mind, the district certainly didn't.

Classes went by. No one had anything to add. Grisson had

relented and scheduled an assembly for the afternoon. I sat with Skates in the balcony of the auditorium, surrounded by excited students. Skates had gotten a good evaluation, falling down only on the score of his relationships with the faculty. Grisson had pointed out that several teachers had taken offense at his heedless remarks and that female teachers especially thought him overly frank in matters relating to sex. He had gotten a job for next year in Los Angeles, where they have a real Jewish community, he told me, and also a real Negro population that understands how to act like one. He was looking forward to it and talked through the first part of the assembly.

On the stage Grisson was giving out awards for the year—for good citizenship, class officers and athletes, and finally for the district-wide spelling contest. He called off the names, waited for the kids to climb up onto the stage, shaking their hands, leading applause and frowning into the audience as The Tribe expressed occasional disbelief in the spelling ability of such-and-such a watermelon-head.

This spelling contest had been a big thing at GW, for they were in competition not only with themselves but with other schools in town. I remembered, a couple of months back, giving out the tests, which arrived all sealed up in big envelopes; we took the tests and got the returns. All those who scored over a certain percentage got to take the next test, and those high enough in that took a third. Those who spelled well enough in the third got the awards up on the stage. They were all ninth-graders from A or B classes.

All except one. After it seemed that all the awards had been distributed, Grisson paused significantly. Everyone waited. Then he said, There is one more spelling award which may come as a little surprise. It is my great pleasure now to call up the last winner in the spelling contest—Leon LaTore.

As Leon LaTore strolled up on the stage, The Tribe went wild. The kids roared out in what seemed to me equal parts of disbelief, astonishment, glee and disgust, keeping it up long after Leon LaTore had shaken Grisson's hand and left the stage. Around us I could see other teachers nodding and smiling; it was another victory—the rebel brought back into the fold, a threat to the system conquered by the carrot. Grisson was leading the way, and everything was OK.

Unfortunately, I was aware that Leon LaTore hadn't ever taken the spelling tests. They were given only in English classes, and Leon LaTore only had one English class—mine; he hadn't been there when I gave it. He hadn't been in any classes then. I suppose Grisson could have called him in and given him the test privately, but it didn't seem likely, nor did it seem likely that Leon LaTore would have come in and taken that test. In any case Leon LaTore couldn't spell anyway.

So why the award? What the hell? Either Leon LaTore forced some good-spelling kid to sign his—Leon LaTore's—name to his own spelling paper, or else the whole thing was rigged. Forget it, said Skates; it's another goddam bargain. I couldn't see that it made a winner out of anyone.

Like many another event that year there wasn't an answer available, but it was the last day and I didn't have to worry about it. Forget you! I said, talking to myself out loud. Two kids in front of me started to giggle. You hear Mr. Hern-don? one of them said to the other. He say, Forget you!

The movie came on then, something about a bullfighter and a kid. The Tribe was restless during it, standing up, talking, scuffling. Occasionally a teacher would get up and jerk some kid out of the auditorium, the kid protesting, Let go my clothes! I was brooding about the position I found myself in. I felt that if I'd been fired up there in the mountains near Yosemite, it wouldn't have mattered much to me. I hadn't thought of that job as a permanent situation or a serious matter. I hadn't considered how to teach, I'd had no goals for my classes—it had been a job. Now, at the end of this year, I was aware I really was a teacher; whether good or bad didn't enter into it. I couldn't remember when I'd worked so hard or concentrated what intelligence and energy I possessed so seriously on any one effort.

In short it seemed unlikely that any other kind of work was going to satisfy me, at least right then, but it seemed even more unlikely that I was going to get another teaching job very soon. It was a kind of bind I wasn't used to.

Around Skates and me the kids stopped scuffling and began to cheer and yell. I looked at the screen. In the movie, the bull had just gored a matador. Two men came out to distract it, and the bull began to chase them around the ring, crashing into the wooden barrier as the men dodged behind it. Time and time again the bull chased and crashed. The kids yelled and laughed and stood up and fell down again helpless with laughter. Hey, Jim! Skates yelled to me. Look, The Tribe likes it! They like it! He was laughing now too, raising his fist and waving it in the air.

Suddenly the lights went on in the auditorium, the film stopped, and Grissum appeared on the stage. He warned them that any further demonstrations of that sort wouldn't be tolerated; if it happened again the film would be stopped and they could return to their classrooms. Sh! said The Tribe.

Let 'em alone! Skates called out loudly from the balcony. Hell, he said to me, it's the first time all year they like something. So let 'em alone. . . .

Well, the lights went back out, the bull chased everyone around the ring, the kids yelled. In time the movie was over, the lights came on, the kids were dismissed, the season was over too, and we all went home.

(45) Epilogue

My older son Jay was almost four when we spent a summer in Mexico. He liked Mexico pretty well, except for the odd habit the Mexican kids had of speaking Spanish. We could see that he soon understood a lot of what they were saying and urged him, as parents will, to speak Spanish, but he always refused. Perhaps he thought it no good to encourage the Mexican kids in their stubborn ways.

A year later, in the normal course, he went to kindergarten back in the United States. He found it mildly disappointing. There were no toys, he said, and when they got to go outside to play, the teacher always went with them.

I was always asking him how things were going at school, and he was always answering, Fine. I pressed for details: What do you guys do there? One day he said, When we get there we line up, then we go in and sit down at our place, then we get up again, then we talk to the flag.

You talk to the flag?

Uh-huh.

I could see he thought the subject closed, but I said, Well, what do you say to the flag?

He turned on the TV. How do I know? he said. They're talking to it in Spanish.

The kindergarten, it seemed, had some odd habits too. Still, you could see he wasn't bothered by it. For the kindergarten didn't require him to talk to the flag himself, or to understand what they were saying to it. All it required of him was that he stand up and look as if he knew what was going on. That wasn't hard, and it didn't take long, and so he didn't mind doing it.

It's now eight years since my season at GW. I spent a year and a half working part time at the post office and substitute-teaching in the city and the suburbs. Fran put in too many hours working in offices—she could have told the girls a thing or two about that paradise. Then one of the schools where I was substituting, a junior high, had a midyear opening and I got the job. I felt grateful to them; they hired me against Grissum's recommendation, and they didn't have to. After two years there I began to think about settling accounts with GW, and I wrote this book. It was finished around the beginning of 1965.

I still work at that school, which is in a suburb. When I first went to work, it had an air of newness. The school was small, the families mostly Jewish and Catholic and well up in the middle economic class, happy with their simple escape from the troubles of the city. For awhile we had a Negro student, a little kid who played the bongos in the talent shows.

Now, in the short time of six years, the population of the suburb has doubled. Those of the original settlers who could afford it have moved on down the road, onto newly excavated, paved and wired hillsides. The city moved out to replace them. Their replacements were more often working-class, spoke more Spanish, were darker, more occasionally black, had more children, fewer dads, collected more welfare, took achievement tests less well.

There were also more of them. For we now have twice as many students, although the size of the school is the same. The kids won't all fit in the multi-use room at once. The teachers won't all fit in the teachers' room at the same time. We seem to have more visits from policemen, and more pinkeye. We also seem to notice a larger percentage of kids who aren't making it.

This last year three teachers and I worked with a special group of kids who, although "testably" bright, read effectively at lower than fourth-grade level—some a lot lower. We could only take 80 kids. There are another 200 who qualify, from all reports. The school population is close to 1,200. Doesn't that remind you of the popular ghetto-school statistic, the one about one-fourth of the students reading at more than two years below grade level? We are beginning to look like a real school. (It is a real school, you watermelon-head! I know it a real school, but I mean it look like it is too!)

Things just move more slowly away from the city. When I first came, our suburban kids were beginning to use the word *tough,* which GW had already abandoned. It took two more years for *boss* to sound right to them, and *bad* never really caught on. It was not until this year that I finally began to hear the immortal *Forget you!* A former student came by to see me the other day, and, among other things, he told me there were a lot more Negroes up at the high school now. A lot more bloods, he said. What did he think about that? OK, he said. In a funny way, he thought he learned a lot from them. Then he laughed. Besides, he said, it makes things more colorful.

Do I give the impression that we have become a Negro school? Or even an "integrated" school? Not at all. If there are 30 Negro kids with us, I'll be surprised. It's still difficult for Negro families to move into this suburb. Perhaps there are a hundred "Latin" types. We are merely more colorful.

But with all this change, you'd imagine we would make a number of changes in our ways, and of course we have. The district, for instance, changed superintendents. The school has changed principals—every two years. Vice-principals have lasted on the average a year and a half. One year we changed half the staff.

Grouping by ability, formerly anathema in the district, has caught on. We group them high, low and average in math and science; English teachers are waiting their turn. Below that we've tried "remedial" classes, and above that, "enrichment." (The remedial kids complain that they ain't learning nothing but that baby stuff, and the enriched that they do the same thing as the other kids, just twice as much of it.) We "experiment" a lot. We teach Spanish experimentally to everyone, then drop it experimentally. We experiment with slow learners, with non-achievers, with core programs, team teaching, with "innovative" programs. These programs, being only "experiments," remain on the fringe of things; the general curriculum, not being an experiment at all, isn't affected by them.

Mainly, our ideas of order have changed. There are too many kids for us to know them all personally, so we spend more time filling out and reading forms in order to learn about kids we don't know. Along with that, we express an urge for standardization. If we don't know the kid, we'll make up for it by knowing that he was taught percentage in the seventh grade, had South America in the sixth.

The eccentric desires of 1,200 students are much less tolerable than those of 600. Having been given too much boiling water, our response is to bottle it tighter and increase the pressure. We constantly discuss important questions: Shall teachers let kids leave the room during class period? Will we let teachers allow gum-chewing in class? Ought we to have one-way corridors? What is the library for? We legislate against running, yelling, eating, tardiness, cosmetics, transistors, classroom parties and free elections. We invent penalties for transgressors; then we must invent another set of penalties for those who won't abide by the first. So that if a kid cuts school, we give him detention. If he cuts the detention, we suspend him from school, thus solving the problem of the kid who doesn't want to come to school.

When I first worked here, you could hear teachers comment, as one man did, If it wasn't for the kids, I couldn't stand this job! Now we spend our faculty meetings dreaming up ways to contain an enemy force.

Settling accounts with GW, I guess, just isn't in the cards. In fact, I see I've been rambling. Members of our staff do the same thing when they talk about the good old days when we had fewer kids, fewer problems, and were more informal, more friendly, sang a less worried song.

What went wrong? In the old days—six years ago—the kids got along with the system. (Would they now, since we have legislated against safety valves?) The kids are different now. Upon reflection, they too come up with the word *deprived*. If more kids can't or won't go along with us, it is because we have more deprived kids. If virtually all the kids from "lower-income" and "minority" groups are in our own low-ability groups, we turn to the counselors, the social workers, the clinics. Them is deprived kids, goes the cry, and someone ought to do something about it.

Deprived of what? Of intelligence? Do we claim that lower-class kids are just naturally dumber than middle-class kids, and that why they all in that dumb class? Naturally not. We have a list. They are deprived of ego strength, of realistic goal-orientation, of family stability, of secure peer relationships; they lack the serene middle-class faith in the future. Because of all that, they also lack self-control, cannot risk failure, won't accept criticism, can't take two steps back to go one forward, have no study habits, no basic skills, don't respect school property, and didn't read "Cowboy Small."

You can add to this list, or you can find another. But what such a list adds up to is something simple: some kids can't take it as well as others.

Some kids can't stand there calmly while they talk to the flag in Spanish. Or they can in kindergarten, like Jay, but can't keep it up in the fourth or seventh grade. If the kids went along with us in the old days, it was for two reasons: first, there were fewer of them and we were able to allow them enough leeway to live; and second, they were white, middle-class kids in America. Not that the system in general was right for them—only that they fit the ideal of America in 1960 without much worry about it, had a richer life-diet outside of school, and so were tough enough to take it.

All right. Some can take it, and some can't. Those who cannot expose the point—it's not any good for anyone. My wife's father was once bitten by a cottonmouth, and survived. Another man from the same community was bitten and died. No one argued that the experience was good for either one of them. Sitting in a classroom or at home pretending to "study" a badly written text full of false information, adding up twenty sums when they're all the same and one would do, being bottled up for seven hours a day in a place where you decide nothing, having your success or failure depend, a hundred times a day, on the plan, invention and whim of someone else, being put in a position where most of your real desires are not only ignored but actively penalized, undertaking nothing for its own sake but only for that illusory carrot of the future—maybe you can do it, and maybe you can't, but either way, it's probably done you some harm.

It's difficult to stop. One always doubts the message is clear enough. I took a ride over by GW the other day, just to take a look. It hadn't changed, that I could see. Now, of course, it won't change for me at all. As far as I'm concerned, Roy and Harvey, Alexandra and Ruth still go there. If I were to work there again, I guess I'd try to do about the same thing, in about the same way, and as often have little idea about how it was going to turn out.

The only thing is, I now know they aren't unique—that GW is not unique. More colorful, no doubt, more vehement in showing us the error of our ways, less cooperative while we talk to the flag, but, as Sullivan said, rather more like the rest of us than less.

What to do? You can read suggestions for change in a lot of recent books by serious and intelligent men. I suppose I could add mine. But frankly, I have almost no hope that there will be any significant change in the way we educate our children—for that, after all, would involve liberty, the last thing we may soon expect—and so I have thought merely to describe one time for you, parents, kids, readers, the way it is.

July 4th, 1967